Tales and Legends From India

BY

M. DOROTHY BELGRAVE

AND

HILDA HART

Illustrated by

HARRY G. THEAKER

RAPHAEL TUCK & SONS, Ltd

*Publishers to Their Majesties the King & Queen
and to H.R.H. The Prince of Wales.*

LONDON · PARIS · NEW YORK

DESIGNED & PRINTED IN ENGLAND

FROM "THE ADVENTUROUS BRETHREN"

HIS NAME IS SATYAVAN
From "The Noose of Fate"

FROM "THE ADVENTURES OF RAMA AND SITA"

CONTENTS

LIST OF COLOUR PLATES

FROM "THE KING'S COLUMN"

6

THE CALL OF THE EAST

HAVE you heard of " The Call of the East ? "
It is heard by those who have lived out yonder,
where the sun rises. It is a call to return to the
blue skies and spice-laden breezes, where the birds
are of the colours of the rainbow, and the butter-
flies and the beetles are as jewels—emeralds, rubies,
and sapphires; where the fireflies flit in the still
and scented night, each with his tiny lamp alight;
where the luscious fruit is had for the picking, and
the flowers are too beautiful to gather; and where
everyday life is as living in Fairyland.

I know there is another side to this picture, but
those who hear the call forget it and remember
only the golden glories.

7

Now, if you get up in the morning and find yourself in Fairyland, and go to bed in Fairyland, just every day as a matter of course, what must the real Fairyland of India be like ?   What must their stories and legends be like, that are told in such rich fancies, and painted in such bright yet beautifully harmonious colours ?

They are here before you for you to judge for yourself, to feast your thoughts on the strange and charming stories, and your eyes on the lovely pictures, and then I am sure you will feel the fascination of the land where the sun rises, and know what those dream of when they hear " The Call of the East."

EDRIC VREDENBURG

FROM " THE ADVENTUROUS BRETHREN "

THE
NOOSE
OF FATE

ONCE upon a time, there was a King who ruled over a large and rich state in India, and he was reputed the best horseman in the whole of his territory. He could curb the fiercest steed and gallop as fast as the wind; indeed, all horses seemed to know directly he approached that he was their master, and because of this power over them he was called Lord-of-Horses.

Now, in spite of his fame and fortune, and the possession of a beautiful Queen, he was never happy, for no children were born to him, and this was accounted a terrible affliction in his country. He wandered from temple to temple, offering sacrifices and praying and weeping, but all was in vain. It seemed as though one or many of the Gods had a grudge against him.

At length he called Narada, his chief counsellor, to him. "You see, Narada," he said, "that though I have been married for five years, I am still without an heir to my throne. By what means can I propitiate the Gods ? "

And Narada, who was a sage and prophet, as well as a counsellor, answered—

"Oh King, the Gods have ever loved the beauty of temples."

Then the Lord-of-Horses smote his hands together, and immediately twelve of his slaves appeared and fell to the earth before him, while he gave his orders.

"Gather together my cunningest workmen, and tell them to build me a temple taller than three tall palm trees. Let it be painted gold within, and gold without ; set a hundred steps of clear white marble before the door, and upon the roof, towers and domes uncountable. Let it be the most marvellous temple ever made by the hands of men, so that Brahma, king of Gods, shall not disdain it." Narada cried, " O Lord-of-Horses, it shall be done ; " and the slaves withdrew.

Before many months had passed the temple raised its shining minarets to the blue sky overhead, and round about it was planted a garden, full of sweet-smelling flowers, and shrubs of magical healing powers, and trees in which brightly plumed birds nested and sang. And every day for the next eighteen years the King visited the sanctuary, making special offerings to Brahma and his wife Savitri, that they might send him a son.

His Queen and his nobles, and even Narada, had quite given up hope, when one day, as the King laid his usual offering on Brahma's shrine, he thought he saw a figure growing out of the flames that consumed his sacrifice. He looked again—surely he was not mistaken. And then he heard a voice—the voice, it must be, of a goddess, for it was sweet in his ear, like the tinkling of distant goat-bells, and, though it was small, it filled the whole of the temple with its sound. " Thou hast pleased me with thy devotion. I am Savitri, wife of Brahma. Ask a boon."

The King scarcely dared to answer, but at last he lifted his trembling face and said, " Goddess, I desire a son, so that my name may not perish from the land." " I will give thee a daughter," replied the clear sweet voice ; and when he again raised his eyes to the shrine the fire had died down, and the sacrifice was consumed, but the ashes had formed themselves into the shape of a tiny baby.

Soon afterwards there was great rejoicing in the

royal palace ; a daughter with hair the colour of the sun, and eyes lovely as the lotus, had been born to the Queen. She was indeed a gift from heaven, so radiantly beautiful that her mother and father could not bear to let her out of their sight, and the courtiers and servants of the palace told each other that she was, in very fact, heaven-born and not a human child at all. Their belief was strengthened when a proclamation went forth that she was to be called " Savitri," after the wife of Brahma, who had promised her to the King.

In course of time Savitri grew from childhood to girlhood, and her father began to think that she should choose a husband from among the princes of the neighbouring states.

" Daughter," he said to her one day, " is it your will to wed ? "

And she answered, " My father's will is mine."

" Go, then," he said, " on a visit to the palaces of our neighbouring Kings, and choose for yourself among the Princes."

He was quite willing to rely upon her judgment, for Savitri had proved herself, during her short life, as wise as she was lovely, and the King knew that she had knowledge of things hidden from him, and powers more than mortal.

It was with a blithe heart that she called her maidens to her, and chose from among them four whom she most trusted. " Prepare my chariot for a long journey," she commanded. " Yoke it to my white oxen, and put upon them their jewelled trappings." But when all was ready, she directed the drivers to seek the paths which led, by a winding, hidden route, to the remote temples of the forest. There, secluded from the gay life of men, dwelt numbers of hermits, who passed their lives in prayer and fasting and good works. Among them Savitri was determined to seek her husband, rather than among the noble friends of her father, most of whom, she knew, would willingly marry her for her wealth, whether they loved her or not.

After many days, the drivers told her that a hermitage was now in sight, so Savitri and her maidens dismounted from the chariot, and humbly approached what looked like a small bare temple, close to the side of which was built a hut of leaves and branches. Inside the hut they found an old, old man, and after conversing with him, and learning much wisdom, they were directed to the next hermitage. In this way they traversed the forest, mingling with saints and sages of every class ; but though these men were all full of virtue, they were also aged and grey and feeble, and Savitri's heart burned within her for youth and strength, as well as goodness.

" Besides," she said, laughing, to her companions, " Brahma would never forgive me if I persuaded one of his votaries to desert the forest and return again to the merry life of cities and palaces."

At length she came to a dwelling rather bigger than the others she had seen, and in the doorway sat a man, old, like most of the forest hermits, but with an air different from theirs. He was, indeed, not a priest, but a King ; and years before he had gone blind, and been driven out of his country by an ancient enemy, who usurped his throne, and threatened instant death should he or any of his family set foot within the land of Shalwa. As Savitri stood watching the blind old man, and wondering how and why he wore his poverty so regally, a youth on a coal-black horse came crashing through the trees, singing a song as he rode :

" The sun shines upon my face : he thinks to sting and pain me ; but his arrows, striking me, cause only laughter upon my lips. To-night I shall behold the moon ; her coolness will satisfy my thirst, and balm from her will fall upon my heart."

" You are dressed like a peasant," said the Princess to herself, " but you sit your steed like a prince, and you sing your song like a poet." And when she caught sight of his face, she too laughed aloud, for she knew that now she had seen her mate.

The youth rode towards the dwelling, dismounted, tethered his horse, saluted the old man tenderly, and presently they both disappeared through the doorway.

" Come, my maidens," said Savitri, " we need travel no further ; let us crave hospitality from these good people, and in a few days we will return home."

Needless to say, the old King of the Shalwas made the maidens welcome, telling them that they might now learn the happiness and content of a peasant's life. He told them, too, of his misfortunes, of how he, and his wife, and their little son Satyavan, had been driven from Shalwa twenty years ago, and had lived ever since among the hermits, safe at any rate from their wicked foe. And, all the time, Satyavan stood in the shadow, watching Savitri, and falling further in love with her every moment. Not many days had passed before they had vowed eternal faith to each other, and she had told him that she must return to her father's kingdom and ask his consent to their marriage, after which she would come back to the forest, and follow him, as her lord, for the rest of her life. "But tell your parents none of this," she said, " until I give you permission."

Savitri arrived at her father's palace on a day when he was holding counsel with Narada; and it happened that the sage was questioning the King about his daughter. "Thou knowest, O lord and master," he said, " that it is the will of Brahma for our children to marry when they are of ripe age."

"Look up, Narada," answered the King, " even now Savitri approaches, and she will tell you whether or not she has found herself a husband."

" Yea, sire, I have," she cried, as she knelt at

2

his feet for blessing. "In his garb and accoutrements he is a poor man's son, in his nature he is a hero, in his birth a prince. He has the face and form of a young god, the simplicity and truth of a peasant."

"And his name, daughter?"

"His name is Satyavan."

More she could not say, for at the word, Narada sprang forward and, raising one hand, solemnly spoke: "No, Princess, not Satyavan."

But Savitri only smiled, and answered, "He, O sage, he and none other."

Then the King begged Narada to explain why the name of the Prince had so moved him.

"Is this youth not noble, brave, and strong? Is he not all that my daughter avers?"

"Indeed, lord and King, he is all that she avers—all and yet more."

"Then is he already betrothed? Is there a curse of the gods upon him? Speak, Narada; I see you know more than we."

Narada bowed his head, and in a low voice uttered the terrible secret. "Fate has set her noose for him. Yama, God of Death, is on his track. Within a year this Prince must die."

For a moment Savitri staggered and blanched. Then a voice within her seemed to whisper,

"Courage! Have not the Gods ears, have they not hearts?" The colour came back to her cheeks, she drew herself up. "Narada, you have prophesied. It is left for me to pray and hope. Not even the knowledge of this doom can shake my purpose. Satyavan shall be my husband for one year, even if for fifty I must mourn a widow."

The sage stood for the space of some moments with his head sunk upon his breast, and his long cloak drawn right over his face. The King and the Princess scarce drew breath, for they guessed he was sunk in some prophetic dream. At length he pushed his cloak back and raised his hands towards Savitri as if in blessing. "Peace attend you, daughter of the Lord-of-Horses," he said, and turned away.

"What means he, Father?" asked the Princess, when his quiet footsteps had ceased echoing down the marble corridors.

"I know not," answered the King. "Be it sufficient for us that he did not forbid your marriage. It is for you, child, to decide your fate. Knowing the curse that rests upon him, will you still wed this forest Prince?"

"I can marry no one else," she answered simply.

The next day it was announced that the Princess of the Lotus Eyes—for so the common people called her—would shortly marry a lord in a far distant territory, and, since the journey was long and tedious, only her father would accompany her thither. Preparations were speedily made, and soon the Lord-of-Horses and his radiant daughter set out alone towards the forest. They drove in the oxen-drawn chariot, and took with them many rich gifts for the mother and father of the bridegroom. But when the King of the Shalwas heard what had brought them to his humble dwelling, he was amazed and, at first, horror-struck.

"How can this be?" he asked. "How will your daughter, the heaven-sent Princess, fare in this rough country? On what shall we feed her? Who will tend on her? We live a peasant's life here, forgetful of jewels and slaves, couches of silk and soft music. We sleep on the hard earth, we eat the berries and fruits of the forest, we clothe ourselves with the skins of beasts and the bark stripped from the trees, and our only pleasure is in abstinence and prayer."

Then Savitri took the blind old man by the hand, and spoke some words of comfort and explanation to him, after which he demurred no longer, but

THE NOOSE OF FATE

"SAVITRI TOOK THE BLIND OLD MAN BY THE HAND, AND SPOKE
SOME WORDS OF COMFORT AND EXPLANATION"

took his guests inside the leafy house and told his wife who they were, and why they had come.

Soon Satyavan returned from hunting, and that same evening Savitri was given him in marriage, many of the hermits who dwelt near coming to bless their union. And all marvelled at the beauty of the Princess, and praised her sweet speech and gentle manners. She pleased her new friends especially by taking off all her jewels, and replacing her rich garments with a brown bark dress such as the forest people wore, " For I am no longer a Princess," she said, " but a poor man's wife."

The Lord-of-Horses presently bade his daughter farewell, and told her that when her year of wifehood was over, she was to come back to her own land and people.

The days slipped by all too quickly, and it seemed to Satyavan that his bride grew lovelier and more gentle every hour, and that there never could have been so happy a man as he. Savitri, too, was happy ; but now and then she would leave the Prince and go away by herself into the depths of the forest, and weep and groan, because of the doom that was approaching ; and at last the time came when the voice she sometimes heard within her, whispering strange truths, told her that her husband had only three more days to live. She decided that if it anyhow lay within her power, she would not leave his side by day or night. " Perhaps I may see Yama as he approaches to lay his noose about my lord ; and I may then forestall him or persuade him, or outwit him." So she watched and waited, and scarcely slept, until the third day dawned. In the morning the old blind father told his son to go out to a certain part of the forest, where he should find some young bamboos. These he should cut, and bring home in preparation for a sacrifice on the following day.

Savitri begged to accompany him and, as she had never before asked any favour, the old man consented, telling her, however, not to hinder the youth in his labours.

Satyavan ran and leapt and whistled, for his heart was light, and he wondered that his bride went so sadly, remembering that, as a rule, she outran and outjested him. Alas ! he little knew how her limbs trembled with fear as she walked, and how she turned her eyes this way and that, searching among the trunks of the trees for the first signs of Yama's approach. They soon reached the spot where the young bamboos grew, and Satyavan raised his axe ; but he had scarcely

lifted it above his head for the first stroke, when it fell from his hands.

"Oh! oh! Savitri," he called to her, "what ails me? Raging pains tear my brain, and the strength has gone from my muscles. Sit down a while and take my head upon your lap, and let me sleep." Then Savitri knew that the fatal moment was at hand. She sat down as he asked her, but his head had only just touched her knee, before she was conscious of a horrible form bending over her. It was tall and gaunt, of a greenish colour, its eyes fiery red, and in its hand it held a long noose of rope.

Savitri knew well that this was Yama, the God of Death, but to give herself space for thought, and to calm herself, she slowly rose from the ground and, bowing low before him, said, " Who art thou, mighty one ? "

" Ask not my name, Savitri," the form replied. " I have come for Satyavan, whose term of life is ended."

And instantly he threw his noose towards the sleeping Prince, and caught his soul in the coils, and drew it right out of his body. Then turning southwards, he fled with lightning speed, hauling the soul behind him. But Savitri was fleeter of foot than any other mortal ; love lent her wings, and she followed close at Yama's heels. They came at last to the edge of the world, beyond which no mortal may pass alive, and here the God stopped and spoke.

" Return, maiden ; you have followed far enough. Return and bury your husband's body with due rites." But Savitri answered, " Nay, great Yama, when I wed my lord I vowed to follow him, wheresoever he was sent or taken. I have done no wrong since I made that vow, and the Gods have therefore no power over me to make me break it."

"You speak the truth," said Yama, "and you have pleased me with your answer. Ask a gift from me—but not the gift of your husband's life."

Savitri thought a moment, and then asked that the old King of the Shalwas should regain his sight and health.

"It is granted," said the God. "Now return; no mortal may pass this spot alive."

Again Savitri refused, and again paused a moment to think. She knew that no one loved Yama, that he was friendless even among the other Gods, so she decided to flatter him. "O Yama, is it true that a mortal is pleasing to the Gods, if she mingles with those who are virtuous?"

"It is true," answered Yama.

"Then you cannot force me to part company with you, for you are virtuous, and I become more pleasing to the Gods—of whom you are one—by staying beside you."

Yama was delighted with this remark, and told Savitri that, for her good sense, she might obtain another gift from him.

"Grant that my father-in-law may regain his lost kingdom," she said. Yama assented, and told her for the third time to go back, and find her husband's body before it should be devoured by jackals. "It matters not at all," replied she, "whether the jackals devour the corpse. Of what use is the body without the soul? Another body could be found for the soul, if it should be released from your noose, but never another soul for the body."

"You speak greater wisdom than I hear from most mortals," said the God. "Yet one more gift will I grant you."

"Grant me a hundred sons, O mighty Yama," she cried; and when the God bowed his head in assent she laughed and clapped her hands. "If you are indeed just and righteous, if you keep your word with men, then release the soul of Satyavan. No other man can I ever wed, and only therefore by giving him back his life, can your third boon be fulfilled."

Yama knew now that Savitri had been allowed, by a power greater than he, to triumph over him, so he unloosened the coil of rope, and Satyavan's soul fled up into the air and back to the forest grove where his body lay. After many hours of travel, Savitri reached the same place, and there she saw her husband lying just as she had left him, seemingly fast asleep. So she lifted his head, and pulled open his eyes, and he stretched himself and yawned.

"Why did you not wake me before?" he asked. "Surely I have slept too long." But Savitri only laughed and kissed him, telling him to come with her quickly, for the sun had set, and darkness was shrouding the land. So hand-in-hand they went back to their forest home, and on the way she told him all that had happened.

When they came in, they found their father and mother rejoicing with some of the hermits because the old man's sight had that afternoon suddenly returned to him ; and even as Savitri was in the midst of relating her terrible adventure, a messenger arrived to say that the King's enemy had been slain, and that the people of the land wished their former and rightful sovereign to return and rule them.

The next day Savitri and Satyavan, with their parents, accompanied the messenger back to Shalwa, and there they all lived prosperously for the rest of their lives. To Savitri were born a hundred sons, as Yama had promised, and on the tenth birthday of each one there was always held a great feast, at the end of which the Queen—for in course of time she and Satyavan ascended the throne—would relate to the whole Court and family, how she had saved the King from the noose of Fate.

" WHO'LL BUY MY MANGOES ? "

WHEN it was known that King Brahmadatta was anxious to marry, kings and princes came from far and wide with their beautiful daughters to visit him. But beautiful as these maidens were, Brahmadatta would choose none of them, and contrived to find objections to each in turn. The first was too talkative, the second too silent, the third too serious, the fourth too scatter-brained, and so on, until every single princess had been rejected.

After the departure of the last high-born maiden Brahmadatta sat in gloomy silence until one of his courtiers ventured to address him.

" O King ! " he said, " since none of these princesses has found favour in your sight, where now will you find a bride worthy of you ? "

" I know not," answered Brahmadatta sadly; "but until my heart is touched I must remain unwed."

The king was reclining, according to his custom, before an open window of the palace where, unseen by his people, he could watch them in the market-place below. The scene was a gay one ; the sun glinting upon shining armour, bales of costly silks and priceless jewels, lent the whole picture a festive air. The humbler tradespeople threaded their way through the crowds, and their voices, shouting their wares, rose harshly on the air. Amongst these voices Brahmadatta could distinguish one—clear as a bell—calling : " Mangoes ! Who'll buy my mangoes ? "

The musical tone pleased him and, searching the crowd until he found its owner, the king's eyes alighted upon Sujata, the daughter of a poor fruiterer, who was busily plying her trade. Lovely as the dawn, her beauty in no way diminished by the rags she wore, Sujata sold her mangoes, quite unconscious of the king's gaze.

" What entrancing beauty ! " cried Brahmadatta, turning to the courtier, and he commanded him to bring the girl before him immediately.

Trembling and with downcast eyes Sujata was led into the royal presence. The king's eyes had not deceived him : Sujata was of surpassing loveliness, and her beauty, simplicity, and modesty so won his heart that he could think and talk of nothing else.

The courtiers put their heads together and whispered : " Surely the king will not marry the daughter of a fruiterer when he has rejected all the high-born in the land. Such a thing would be impossible ! "

But this was exactly what Brahmadatta intended to do. The day after his interview with Sujata he declared : " If I searched my kingdom from end to end I could not find a more perfect wife." So Sujata, a little afraid of the honour thrust upon her, consented to wed the king, and the marriage was celebrated with all due pomp and ceremony.

For a while the king and queen lived together in perfect harmony, yet before many months had elapsed Brahmadatta noticed a disquieting change in his wife. Radiant as ever, Sujata still dazzled his eyes with her beauty, but the simplicity and deference of her demeanour, which had charmed him at first, had vanished, leaving her cold and haughty. Her anger when anything displeased her was vented upon her frightened servants, many of whom had already been dismissed for the most trifling offences.

It was not until the second anniversary of their wedding day, however, that the king's patience was finally exhausted. He had commanded a banquet in honour of his queen, and they sat side by side eating of the rare dishes placed before them. Brahmadatta talked gaily to his friends, but Sujata sat silent and disdainful, scarcely uttering a word, even to the king. Some trifle had displeased her before the banquet, and she was in no mood to be amiable. Towards the end of the meal, dishes of fruits were placed before the guests—pomegranates, luscious pears, mangoes, dates, figs, and others too numerous to mention.

The king, with his own hands, placed a fine mango upon Sujata's plate.

"What is this thing?" inquired the queen coldly. "Am I expected to eat it?"

Brahmadatta could hardly believe his own ears.

"So it has come to this, has it?" he shouted. "You seek to forget who you were before I made you a queen. Proud and scornful woman, I discovered you selling mangoes in the market-place, and to the market-place you shall return. There you may learn again what a mango is. Go, for I will have nothing more to do with you!'.

Sujata, cowed and trembling, left the feast, and from that day nothing more was heard of her.

Brahmadatta had intended never to see her again, but he had reckoned without his affection. Life without his beautiful queen became impossible. He completely forgot her recent faults and only remembered her charm and simplicity in the early days of their marriage. After a while his longing for Sujata grew unbearable and he sent

3

messengers into the city to find her and to beg her to return to him. But Sajuta was not to be found. She had vanished from the royal city and none knew whither she had gone.

Then Brahmadatta set out upon a journey in search of her, and after many days he came upon a market-place in a strange city. Amid the din of voices his ears caught the well-known cry: "Mangoes! Who'll buy my mangoes?" To his joy, there was Sujata in the crowd. She was dressed in rags, as of old, and her beauty was dimmed with the traces of privation and recent tears, but in the eyes of Brahmadatta she was as lovely as ever.

Hastily borrowing a cloak from one of his attendants, Brahmadatta approached Sujata, hiding his face in the garment. "What have you there, maiden?" he asked in a feigned voice.

"Mangoes, fine mangoes, sir," she answered.

"O Sujata!" cried the king, throwing aside his disguise, "now that you have remembered what a mango is, I pray you come back with me to my kingdom." Sujata fell at his feet, begging his forgiveness for her folly, and the king raised her and embraced her tenderly.

Then they returned to the palace of Brahmadatta, and thenceforward the queen was as kind and gentle as the king could desire.

THE ADVENTUROUS BRETHREN

PART I

THE RIVAL ARCHERS

LONG years ago there ruled over a great part of India, an ancient King called Bhishma. He was really much too old for his duties, but of his sons, the elder, Dristarastra, was blind; and the younger, Pandu, was dead; so until the children of these two grew up, and were able to take over kingly duties, their white-haired grandfather was obliged to act both as their guardian, and protector of the realm.

The heir of Dristarastra was named Duryodhana—a brave but envious and ambitious youth— and he and his many brothers were called

"Kurus;" while Pandu's children, five only in number, were known as the "Pandavas." Yudhishthira was the eldest ; then came Bhima ; next Arjuna, who, even as a baby, showed remarkable strength and fearlessness ; and last, the twins, who always played, worked, laughed and cried together.

Now old Bhishma was very anxious that the two families of cousins should be trained in every branch of princely accomplishment ; but, try as he might, he had not yet found any one really fit to teach them the whole art of warfare, and he was beginning to grow anxious on this score, for Duryodhana and Yudhishthira were now approaching the years of manhood, and were still mere babes in the use of arms.

One day, however, the lads discovered a teacher for themselves—and a fortunate discovery it was.

They were playing near a well, and one of them kicked their ball, which was painted exquisitely with pictures of monkeys, tigers and other forest creatures, right into the water. With sticks and stones they tried to recover it, but only succeeded at length in making it sink to the bottom. They were about to give up their toy as lost for ever, when Arjuna, favourite among the Pandavas, spied a priest sitting cross-legged on the ground not far away, and looking earnestly towards them.

" Let us ask that old Brahman," he said to the others. " Grandfather Bhishma has often told us that a good priest can work magic. Perchance he can direct us how to get back our ball."

So the lads trooped up to the old man, and telling him their trouble, were reassured when he smiled at them and solemnly nodded his head. But then he assumed a grave expression and frowned.

" Fie, little princes ! " he said. " Are you indeed the famous Kurus and Pandavas, sons of the Royal house, and can you not perform so simple a task as to shoot up a ball from the depths of a well ? Fie ! fie ! Who is your master of archery ?"

" We have none," answered the lads. " But, good sir priest, is it possible to shoot up our lost ball ? Show us how ! Show us how ! "

Upon this the Brahman pulled a ruby ring from his finger, and threw it after the ball.

" There," he said, " not only will I bring back your toy, but my ring also " ; and, to the amazement of the princes, he plucked a handful of grass, and, selecting a blade, aimed it with great precision at the ball, which was clearly to be seen some fifty feet below in the water. The blade of grass pierced the ball as though it had been a needle piercing silk; and the sage then threw another blade, which struck through the upstanding end of the first one; then another and another, until he had formed a perfect chain of grass, by means of which he easily pulled the ball to the surface.

The princes watched this performance with held breath. " Good, good ! " and " Oh, wise and clever Brahman ! " they shouted in chorus. " Now bring up the ring ; bring up the ring ! "

Immediately the priest took his bow, and carefully choosing an arrow from his quiver, shot it into the water. Imagine the amazement and delight of the onlookers when, in a second, the dripping arrow returned to the hand that had loosed it, bearing upon its feathered end the ruby ring.

The boys clapped their hands and leapt round and round. This magic was even more fascinating than that of the travelling fakirs, with their dancing serpents and the swords that they swallowed whole ! But Yudhishthira, eldest of the Pandavas, silenced the hubbub, and, pushing his way to the front, asked the Brahman what return he and his comrades could make for such a wonderful exhibition of skill.

" Tell thy grandsire, the mighty Bhishma, that Drona, who wields the bow as well as he the sceptre, has travelled many miles, and is now hungry and in need of water."

The lads scampered to the palace with the message, and broke in upon the King, each anxious to be the first to deliver it, and to enlarge upon the prowess of their newly-found friend.

" Drona here ! " exclaimed Bhishma, when he heard the news. " Go out quickly, my sons, and bring him hither." But he had scarcely spoken when two slaves drew back the rich hangings before the portal of the chamber, and the Brahman appeared. He bowed low before the King, and then seated himself cross-legged upon the floor, and rested his head on his hands.

" Welcome, Drona," said the old sovereign. " Never before have I seen thee, but the fame of thy skill with weapons, and of thy exceeding holiness, has travelled to me. Wherefore hast thou sought me out ? "

" Give me private audience, oh Bhishma," cried the priest, " and I will unfold my story."

Whereupon, the chamber being cleared, he continued : " In the days of my youth, oh King, I was nurtured and trained up with princes, and the sons of princes. Among the dearest of my comrades was Drupada, now King of Panchala, and he and I, ere we parted, swore a boyish oath each to the other, of eternal friendship, fidelity, and mutual assistance, if need arose.

" Now, I, after these early years, devoted myself to a life of holiness and poverty, giving up all my

possessions and
living in the
forests amidst
the hermits.
But after some
years I married
and had a son,
for whose sake I
determined to
return again to
the world and
the life of cities.
In my need I
went first to
Drupada, and
asked him for
money and
clothes, until
such time as I
could find pupils
enough to in-
struct in the use
of weapons—for

even in the forests I had not let my heaven-sent
skill rust disused. And Drupada scornfully sent
me away, saying that it was not meet for a King
to speak with a poor priest, and that he had no

knowledge of me, nor had he ever heard of the name of Drona.

" Therefore, oh Bhishma, have I vowed that he shall remember my name with sorrow and tears, but the time of my revenge is not yet, and, until the day dawns, I must needs turn schoolmaster. I heard thou wert in need of such an one, for thy grandsons."

Bhishma replied that Drona might, from this moment, live in the palace and regard himself as chief tutor to the Kuru and Pandava brethren, who, to say the truth, had been eagerly hoping for this end to their adventure of the morning.

The next day Drona took the youths to a clearing in the forest, and, before the first lesson began, he commanded them to seat themselves in a circle round him. He then solemnly asked them whether, if he taught them the use of every kind of weapon, so that they should become more skilled to attack and defend than any other princes in India, they would in return promise some day to carry out a certain plan he was treasuring in his heart.

More than that he would not tell them, and most of them, fearing what the plan might be, shook their heads wisely, and Duryodhana was heard to murmur something about the foolishness of a blindfold promise.

But Arjuna of the Pandavas sprang up from the circle and swore aloud that whatever Drona should in the future ask him to do, that he would perform.

Then Drona drew the lad to him and kissed him on the brow ; after which it seemed that a special bond existed between these two, Drona ever watching his pupil as keenly and lovingly as a father, and Arjuna staying closer to his master than the others, and hanging on every word of instruction that issued from those pious lips.

Before long, such was Arjuna's devotion that he had outstripped all his companions and could handle his weapons, especially his bow and arrow, almost as well as Drona himself.

One night they had pursued their lessons and practice in the forest until the sun sank, and they found themselves some way from home when darkness swept down on them. So Drona told them to sit, and gave each boy some rice and fruit, lest he should faint with hunger after the day's exercise. As Arjuna ate his portion, he began wondering why his hand so easily found its way to his mouth, though he could see nothing.

" It is because my hand is so used to the

journey," he thought. "And why should not that same hand learn to string a bow, and shoot towards a sound, without the help of the eye?" So he leapt up, and began practising in the dark, aiming at birds who sat chirruping on the trees about.

Drona heard the twang of the bow-strings, and, coming to him, embraced him, telling him that the name of Arjuna, the archer, should one day ring through the world.

Duryodhana was standing near. He had long felt envious of his cousin's skill, and he now ground his teeth with anger. " If I cannot match thee myself," he thought, "I will never rest till I have found a champion to outdo thee. Arjuna the archer, indeed! How I hate thee!" and the jealous youth's anger grew bitterer, even as Arjuna's prowess daily increased.

Now, though Drona was employed by King Bhishma, many princes and nobles from neighbouring territories were permitted to join the classes, the King having no apprehension that any rival youths could attain greater skill than his own grandsons. And among the newcomers was one lad called Karna, of sad and silent character, about whom little could be said except that he looked and spoke as if of noble blood. No one knew the name of his father or mother, but Drona accepted him for a pupil, and therefore his appearance among the others was never challenged, though many were the speculations and stories circulated about him.

From the day of his arrival he showed truly marvellous talent with all manner of weapons, and, by dint of constant attention to his master's lessons, he quickly outstripped his comrades, until it was doubtful whether he were not as brilliant as Arjuna himself; and the two became keen though good-natured rivals.

As soon as Duryodhana perceived this, he did

everything in his power to make friends with Karna, and gave him as a present, on one day alone, a ruby and an emerald, a purse of rupees, a young elephant, and an ebony box of great value carved with a thousand figures, and exuding, when opened, the scent of spices.

Karna was naturally won over by these attentions from the eldest of the Kuru princes, and soon Duryodhana was trying to fan the harmless rivalry which existed between him and Arjuna into a feeling of hostility and hatred. He did not succeed very well at first, but gradually the pupils noticed that the silent youth scarcely ever spoke to the Pandavas, and kept more and more with the Kurus.

At length Drona decided that he would test the skill which his pupils had acquired, by an open competition in archery. So he procured an artificial bird and had it placed on the top of a high tree. Then he assembled his class, and said to them : " Stand in a circle thirty paces away from this tree, and be ready to shoot one by one. Look at the bird on the topmost branch. You are to shoot at his head and try to cut it off."

In great excitement the boys arranged themselves, each one practising his aim and hoping he might be the first to accomplish the task.

" Since he is the eldest of the noble princes assembled," went on Drona, " Duryodhana shall be the first to try." Duryodhana stood steady and raised his bow.

" Tell me, Prince," called his master, " do you see the bird ? "

" I do," replied Duryodhana.

" What exactly do you see ? Your comrades, or me, or the tree, or the bird ? "

" I see all that you name, master ; I see the bird, and the tree, and you and my companions."

" Put down your bow, Prince, and stand aside. You cannot compete."

Wondering what he had said or done to be thus disqualified, Duryodhana moved back, scarcely able to brook his bitter shame and disappointment, for he felt sure that he could have beheaded his target.

One by one Drona called upon his pupils. They were all asked the same question and they all gave the same answer—" Yes, master, we see you and our friends, the tree, and on the top of the tree, the bird." At last all were disqualified except Karna and Arjuna, who, as the champions, had been kept till last. The tears were streaming down old Drona's face, such was his vexation, that none of his pupils had stood this very simple test.

" Alas ! " he cried ; " have I laboured so many months to such poor purpose ? Come, Karna ; either by you or Arjuna must the arrow be shot, or Drona will bury his weapons in the forest, and own himself shamed before all the court."

Karna raised his bow and drew the string taut.

" What see you ? " asked his master.

" I see the tree and the bird, sir," he replied.

" Stand back ; thou canst not shoot. Arjuna, try thou. Dost thou, too, see the tree and the bird ? And me, perchance also, and thy comrades ? "

" Nay," answered Arjuna quickly. " I can see neither them nor thee ; I cannot see the tree nor the branch ; only the bird."

" Describe the bird to me," said Drona in a trembling voice.

" I cannot, master, for I perceive only its head."

" Then shoot," cried the old man exultingly, and Arjuna loosed an arrow, which whirred upward, and severed the head clean from the bird's body.

Drona turned to the others and spoke : " How often, oh my pupils, careless apes that ye are, have I told you that no man can hit if he let his eyes dance from his aim. Ye saw two things, three, four—Arjuna but one. Therefore doth Arjuna ever strike his mark : therefore is Arjuna champion among you all."

The youths then realised how foolish had been their answers, and loudly applauded the Pandava hero; only Duryodhana drew Karna aside and said to him : " Are we always to be worsted by this ' champion '? Perchance Drona, since he loves him so, told him the trick before the trial began."

But Karna answered, " Nay, Prince, wrong not our master. Arjuna has won quite justly; but at the next contest, look you, he shall *not* win."

And after that he worked more earnestly than ever, rising in the night to study books upon the management of weapons, and even practising in the heat of the day, when the others slept ; while ever at his ear whispered the malicious counsels of Duryodhana, poisoning his mind against the noble house of the Pandavas.

4

PART II

THE HOUSE OF LAC

BY the time Drona had been instructor at the palace for three years, he thought that his pupils, especially Arjuna, should be ready to perform the task which, from the beginning, he had destined for them. So having first consulted King Bhishma and gained his consent to the enterprise, he assembled the Princes and thus addressed them :

" For three years, my pupils, have I diligently taught you the whole art of warfare, and never have I required a fee of you. If you would repay me in some measure, band yourselves together and seek out Drupada, King of Panchala, who in past

50

years grievously insulted me. Bind him and bring him to me."

The idea of a raid and some fighting in real earnest, filled the young men with excitement. They collected weapons, chariots, elephants, and as many followers as would bring their full strength up to nine hundred ; and, with Drona in their midst, they set out for the kingdom of the Panchalas, which they reached after three days' journey.

They rode peaceably enough through their enemy's country, giving out that they were on a pilgrimage to the King, until they reached the capital. As soon as they had passed the gates, they drew their weapons and made a rush for the Royal palace, hoping to surprise Drupada and seize him before the guard could be called out. Drupada, however, heard that a company of apparent raiders was in the city, and, hastily arming, he summoned his bodyguard and issued to meet them, expecting only a handful of ruffians who should easily be overpowered.

And, indeed, when he first caught sight of them, they seemed to justify no better a description, for the Kurus, led by Duryodhana and Karna, had completely lost their heads in the excitement, and were riding here, there and everywhere, shouting, laughing, and slashing in all directions without either method or control.

Arjuna, who had taken command of the Pandava division, seeing that his fellows would never come off victors in such a scrimmage, held his men in reserve, and watched the fray. Drupada's well-trained band came steadily forward, and met each excited attack of the Kurus with a firm front, so that before long the invaders found themselves scattered and disorganised ; and with both their leaders wounded, and unable to reform their ranks, they turned and fled back.

Now was Arjuna's chance. With a cry of encouragement to his men, he darted forward ; the twins, on either side, protecting his chariot wheels, and his brother Bhima running in front, armed with a mace and dealing death wherever he struck. Arjuna himself stood upright on the seat of his car, showering arrows in every direction, and at the same time commanding the attack.

For a few moments the battle swayed evenly, but Drupada's force had not been prepared for a second assault, and soon they gave way before the impetuous Pandavas, the King only continuing to fight amid the hail of arrows that descended on him. As soon as Arjuna was within a few yards of the royal chariot, he leapt from his own, and, throwing aside his bow, gripped the King's sword, and deftly wrenched it from his hand.

"Now thou art our prisoner," said the youth, "but thy life is safe unless Drona desires otherwise."

At the mention of the name, Drupada blanched, and when he was led to the warrior-priest, who had been raised shoulder high by the victorious Pandavas, he bowed his head in shame, remembering the vow of his boyhood and the faithless manner in which he had broken it.

"Fear not, and hang not thy head, Drupada," said Drona. "I harbour no vengeance against thee. But since thou wilt admit none but kings to thy friendship, take thou from this day one half only of the kingdom of Panchala, and I will take the other. Then, both being rulers, perchance we can be comrades also."

There was nothing for Drupada to do but accept these terms, at any rate for the moment, so he assented with what appeared to be good grace; and in due time found himself lord of that part of his former territory which lay south of the Ganges, while Drona bade farewell to his pupils and proceeded to take up the kingship of that part which lay to the north.

With sad hearts, the band of young warriors turned their steps homewards, realising that, now Drona had left them, their pleasant forest fellowship would be broken up, and that schooldays must give place to the serious business of life.

Arjuna headed the company, in virtue of his

proven leadership and success; and as they travelled they sang songs of his prowess, to shorten the journey:

" How have the gods blest the house of the Pandavi!
    Lo! Arjuna is one of the brethren; he who can loose fifty
        arrows at once from a single string! He who can fight
        with all manner of weapons! He who conquered the
        Panchalas, and stood aloft above the warriors like a
        palm-tree golden in the sun! "

At the tail of the party rode Duryodhana and Karna; and as they listened to the song, their heads sank lower on their breasts, and frowns of anger and shame clouded their noble countenances. " Revenge! " whispered Duryodhana. " The time will come," answered his companion; and no other word did they speak until at length they arrived at the Court of Bhishma.

The people of Hastinapura had heard by messenger of the brilliant achievements of the Pandavi, and they had decorated the streets and houses with flags, ribbons and flowers to welcome their return; indeed, so popular had the five brethren become that King Bhishma thought it a suitable moment to nominate Yudhishthira crown prince, and to bestow public honours and privileges upon the others.

These marks of favour wrought their elder

cousin to such a pitch of jealousy that he decided, by fair means or foul, to get rid of his rivals without delay. So he approached his father, the blind Dristarastra, who was thoroughly weak and pliable. "You see, father," he said, "that I and my brothers stand no chance of popularity or preferment while our cousins remain at Court. Our grandfather dotes upon Yudhishthira, and Arjuna, with his braggardry and show, has won the sheep-hearts of the people. They have already been given suzerainty over the richest of our provinces, and soon, no doubt, the whole kingdom will be divided among them. Once they find themselves in power it will go hard with the Kurus, for whom, since childhood days, they have ever harboured a secret grudge and enmity." With these and such-like speeches he plied his father, until at length Dristarastra had agreed to a plan by which the Pandavi should be sent away to a distant part of India—"when," thought Duryodhana, "I will devise some means to destroy the whole verminous breed." But of this last wickedness he breathed no word to any man, not even to Karna, who, he knew, would not adopt any underhand means against his rivals.

Before long, news was spread abroad in the

THE PALACE OF LAC
From "The Adventurous Brethren"

Court that a most wonderful festival was to be celebrated at Benares, throughout the coming year : the like of it had never been seen before and would never be seen again. A certain number of the courtiers, secretly instructed by Duryodhana and his father, could talk of nothing else. They described the beauties of the city, dwelling upon the magnificence of the public buildings, the richness of the inhabitants, the gaiety and brilliance of the social life ; until one day Arjuna exclaimed laughingly, " By the god Shiva, whose festival this is to be, it were a pity to die without having set eyes upon such a sovereign city ! " Whereupon Dristarastra quickly turned to King Bhishma and called to him, " Hearest thou the plaint of Arjuna thy grandson ? He desires to go to Benares, to witness the coming sacrifices of Shiva there."

" Go, then, my son," replied Bhishma, " and take with thee thy brethren, if it pleases them."

The idea was acceptable enough to the Pandavi, who had no suspicion that Dristarastra and his son, together with a dozen courtiers in their pay, had been working for weeks to achieve this end. Accordingly they made ready for the journey, taking with them a caravan full of jewels, another of rupees, and five of rich raiment, so that they

should be able to establish themselves in Benares with the splendour which became their rank.

A minister of the Court, named Purochanna, was sent ahead of them, to find a suitable palace and make arrangements for their reception. Little did Bhishma think, as he gave his consent to the departure of this emissary, that he had been bribed by Duryodhana to build with all speed a palace of lac, a very inflammable kind of wood, which, if a spark so much as touches it, will turn to a mountain of fire in a few moments.

"Fill the palace with all kinds of the costliest furniture," Duryodhana had said: "spare no expense or trouble, and when you return my father will bestow on you riches greater than you can dream of."

Purochanna's cupidity conquered his conscience, and, breathing no word of the dastardly plot, he set out for Benares, and here fulfilled in detail all the instructions of the wicked Prince. What a terrible fate would have awaited the noble Pandavi, had not there been at the Court a certain Vidura, their mother's brother, who was as wise as he was good, and who, having for a long time suspected Duryodhana, had made it his business to find out by secret means the plots and machinations of the Prince !

Before the Pandavi started on their journey, therefore, he took them to his private chambers and, setting a guard outside doors and windows for fear of espionage, he told them that dangers of the most appalling kind awaited them, and that a scheme was afoot against their lives. Their best course, he said, would be to appear, for the present, innocent of their enemies' devices ; and that he would, from time to time, keep them informed of what was happening at Court, and help them to escape when the fate which threatened them approached.

The whole city turned out to send the five brothers triumphantly on their way ; flowers were thrown upon them from all the balconies, and " The blessings of Shiva upon ye," re-echoed from street to street.

Duryodhana, contrary to his usual sulky habit,

was most fervent in his good wishes, boisterously laughing and shouting songs as he rode beside them. Old Bhishma accompanied them to the city gates in his golden chariot drawn by black oxen; and when the time came to say farewell, he wept as he kissed each of the noble youths, and gave them his blessing, reminding them to return, without fail, at the end of the twelve months' festival.

Vidura rode with them some way beyond the city, and, before he parted, spoke to Yudhishthira in a low voice, and in a language known only to those two.

"Guard yourselves from surprise both by day and night. Forget not that your enemies only wait their opportunity. Study the forest tracks that lead from Benares hitherward, and learn to guide yourselves by sun and stars. When a man comes to you with implements for mining, close not your doors to him; and remember that a trading ship with a red mast, plying the Ganges, will not prove an enemy to you." And, gravely embracing the Prince and his brothers, the good Vidura turned his horse's head back towards Hastinapura.

When the Princes arrived in Benares they were received with great acclamation by the people, for their fame had travelled everywhere.

Purochanna was among the first to make his salaams, and ceremoniously informed them that, as he had been unable to find a house sufficiently splendid, he had employed workmen by day and night, to erect a palace, which, he said, was now ready equipped with costly furniture, with slaves, musicians, dancing girls, and every other luxury necessary for the comfort and con-venience of his young masters.

The Pandavi appeared delighted with this news; but on arriving at the palace, they all noticed that the smell of tar, oil, and other inflammable substances was ill-concealed by that of the strong scents and spices which had been lavishly scattered everywhere.

For eleven months the brethren remained in their dangerous habitation, but so shrewdly did they guard it that none of Duryodhana's agents obtained a chance of carrying out his fell orders, which were, to burn the palace to the ground one night when it was certain that the Princes were asleep within.

At the beginning of the twelfth month a man arrived at the palace entrance and demanded audience with Yudhishthira, presenting to the guard and servants a ring, which, he said, would instantly gain him admission when the prince beheld it. Upon the ring was graven a symbol, unintelligible to the gaping curiosity of those who carried the message; but to Yudhishthira the marks meant " Friend," in the secret language of Vidura. He therefore ordered the stranger into his presence, and found that he had brought with him various mining tools, with which, he said, he proposed to make a subterranean passage leading from the back of the buildings into the forest beyond; and by means of this any one could easily escape in case of fire.

As soon as the passage was complete, Arjuna's restlessness knew no bounds.

" I am weary of this life in Benares, brothers," he said. " It seems that we have outwitted our

"A HOUSE EQUIPPED WITH COSTLY FURNITURE, WITH SLAVES, MUSICIANS AND DANCING GIRLS"

63

enemies, or that their courage does not rise to their desire for our destruction. Since they cannot, or will not, burn us out of this palace, which, to me, has become little better than a prison, let us take the brand from their hands, and burn ourselves out."

At first Yudhishthira would pay no attention to this wild scheme; but at length he, too, grew weary, and longed once more to look upon his aged grandfather, and his good uncle Vidura, and to see the sparkling turrets and arcades of Hastinapura. So one night, having on one pretext or another, sent all their servants into the city, the Pandavi brethren set fire to the front part of the dwelling, and hastily running through the corridors to the back, they entered the subterranean passage. In a few moments the whole palace was blazing, and the citizens ran from all parts of the town to watch the great fire, for the spires of it seemed to reach almost to the sky, and the heat of it was a hundred times the heat of the sun, when he scorches the earth in summer, so that beasts and men perish beneath his rays.

And the watchers sent up a great wailing, for they deemed that the noble youths had been burned alive before help could reach them.

Meantime, however, the Pandavi had threaded

the mazes of the dungeon passage, and emerged safely into the forest, the tracks and fastnesses of which they had acquainted themselves with during the past year ; and after travelling many miles, they at length came to the banks of the Ganges.

How to cross the river seemed, indeed, a problem, as their fame was so great that they would certainly be recognised if they tried to charter a boat, and they wished it to be believed for the present that they had perished in the House of Lac. They were about to turn and

5

hasten back into cover of the forests, when they saw a vessel with a red mast moored not far away.

The words of Vidura flashed into Yudhishthira's mind: "Brothers," said he, "never trust me if this vessel and its captain be not at our service;" and approaching the ship, he shouted a secret word, to which the captain replied by sending off a small boat to fetch them. He was, indeed, an agent of their uncle's, and had been stationed many months at or near that spot, waiting for the Princes to come.

With light hearts the youths crossed to the other side of the river, and after many adventures they at length settled in the town of Ekachakra, where, disguised in garments of deerskin, with strings of sacred beads hung round their necks, and their hair grown long and matted, they gave out that they were Brahmans come from a long pilgrimage. And so noble was their bearing, and so great seemed their learning, that all and sundry gave them food and alms; and thus they lived, waiting to hear news of their enemies, and confident that before long Vidura would seek them out and advise them how most safely they could set about regaining their position in Hastinapura.

PART III

THE GAMBLER'S WIFE

THE Pandavi had not settled long in Ekachakra when messages were secretly brought to them from friends in their own country. From these they learned that every one in Hastinapura, except their Uncle Vidura and a few trusted followers, believed them to have perished when the House of Lac was destroyed; that Duryodhana had seized all power into his own hands, had pushed both Bhishma and Dristarastra into the background, and was virtual ruler; and that it would be wisest, for the present, for them to remain in hiding.

At length, however, their adventurous instincts awoke again, and when they heard that Drupada, the enemy of Drona, was about to hold a contest, the winner of which should be given his lovely daughter Draupadi in marriage, they decided to attend the ceremony in their Brahman disguise, hoping that some excitement would come their way.

Now Drupada had decided that the cleverest and strongest archer in the land should win his daughter, so he had caused a bow to be made, of wood stiff as iron, and a ring to be hung upon a very tall and slender pole, so that it perpetually swayed in the wind. Whichever suitor should first string the bow, and then shoot five arrows through the ring, should be the chosen bridegroom.

Of course hundreds of nobles thronged to the capital, eager to adventure for the princess, who was known to be rich, beautiful, and good ; and on the appointed day the city was choked with sight-seers as well as competitors. Little models of the great bow had been cunningly fashioned in gold by the smiths, and were being vended in the streets as favours. Flower girls were selling posies and garlands. Beggars were asking alms, blessing those who gave, cursing those who refused. Bands of soldiers from time to time paraded the main thoroughfares to keep order. And from the steps of twenty temples situated in different districts, heralds announced the conditions under which the contest would shortly open—the chief being that only men above a certain caste, and having ducal blood in their veins, would be allowed to enter the lists.

At last the moment arrived, the arena was thrown open, and princes of all ages crowded to the golden daïs, on which lay the mighty bow ;

while the onlookers pressed eagerly forward to watch the first attempt. Close to the testing spot stood five men dressed as Brahmans, and many looks of admiration, but none of recognition, were cast towards their brawny figures and handsome faces! Presently the Princess Draupadi was seen emerging from a silken pavilion not far away, and five pairs of eyes eagerly scanned her. " By the gods," whispered Yudhishthira beneath his breath, " a maiden worth winning! What a Queen would she make for me! Never saw I so fair a face! " And Arjuna whispered back, " You speak truly—and she shall be ours! "

One by one the competitors tried, and failed, to string the bow, and each time the five seeming Brahmans smiled triumphantly at one another. But their smiles changed to looks of apprehension when the heralds announced a new-comer— Karna, champion of the Kuru princes. Unconscious that ten eyes were darting enmity towards him, he strode up to the daïs and seized the vast weapon. " Now will Draupadi be won," muttered Arjuna. " The curse of the gods upon Karna; I looked not to have seen him here."

The champion strained at the unyielding wood, his muscles stood out, the sweat poured from his face. Would he succeed? The crowd held their

breath. Yes— the straight line was turning to a curve; rounder and rounder it grew. Would the hero support such a strain long enough to loop the string to the upper end, or would his muscles crack with the tension? Allah be praised! He had strung the bow! A tremendous shout rent the air, and it was redoubled when Karna, after several failures, at length shot five arrows through the pendulous and swaying ring. " Karna of the

Kurus is victor," cried the people. "Karna shall wed Draupadi."

The Pandavi groaned, as they saw their hated cousin Duryodhana spring out from the concourse of princes, and taking Karna by the hand, lead him up to the Princess, who was now seated in her bridal robes upon a jewelled throne, just within the entrance to her silken pavilion.

Then a strange thing happened. They saw Draupadi rise and turn inquiringly to Duryodhana. She spoke in a clear voice. "Tell me, Prince, who is the father of your champion? You know that one of the conditions of the contest is that the competitors be of a certain caste. Methinks I have somewhere heard that the father of this Karna was a charioteer, and if that be so, I cannot accept him."

Now Duryodhana did not know what was the parentage of Karna, for, since the days of his pupilage with Drona, the secret of his birth had been well kept. So, abashed, he kept silent, looking towards the youth for an explanation. But Karna only shook his head.

"Go, then," said the Princess; "your suit has failed."

The blood mounted to Karna's cheeks, and he was seen to clench his hands and cast his eyes towards the sun. Then hastily he turned away, and, followed by Duryodhana, was lost to sight in the crowd. At this Arjuna could hold himself back no longer. He strode towards Draupadi, and cried out, " I am of noble lineage, fair Princess, though my garb and looks may proclaim otherwise. Give me leave to test my strength."

Draupadi bowed her head in assent, and before the astonished assembly the great Brahman lifted the bow with one hand, and with the other bent it as though it had been a reed, strung it with dazzling swiftness, and winged five arrows, steady as birds in flight, through the ring which hung aloft.

The crowd broke into wild applause, and the Princess smilingly said, "By your voice, your manner, and knightly prowess, fair sir, your lineage proclaims itself. You have won Draupadi."

The King at first looked somewhat askance at the victor ; but when he learnt that he was none other than Arjuna, champion of the Pandavi, he embraced him. " Ah, Prince ! " he said, " ever since you and your brethren raided my city on behalf of Drona, it has been my secret wish that my daughter should marry one of the famous five ; for though you fought against me, yet was the manner of your fighting that of heroes beloved by the Gods. Indeed, I am blessed in this match above my deserving." And when he found that not Arjuna but the Prince Yudhishthira, heir-apparent of Hastinapura, was to be the bridegroom, his joy knew no bounds. As for Draupadi, she was equally delighted to think that she was to wed the chief of the Pandavi house, and that one day she would be a Queen. So the wedding was celebrated without delay.

The secret, of course, was now out. The news spread like wild-fire that the Pandavi brethren were alive and well, and allied by marriage to the King of the Panchalas.

As soon as old Bhishma heard the tale, he held a council, and said that, in his opinion, his five grandsons must be recalled, and that Duryodhana must resign to them at least one half of the kingdom, over which he had gradually asserted his power, until he had become practically a despot.

Duryodhana could think of nothing at the moment to gainsay this proposal, since all the nobles and even the blind Dristarastra supported it. But by cunning and bribery he so arranged matters that he was to retain the prosperous and populous part of the country, while his cousins were to be given as their share a dismal tract, mostly desert, sparsely peopled, undeveloped and barren. The Pandavi, obeying their grandfather's summons to return, were somewhat dismayed to learn that their cousin's machinations had succeeded so well, and that they were for a second time to be practically banished.

However, they would not for a moment have disputed the arrangements of Bhishma, and, determined to make the best of their bargain, they started off for the largest town—and that a puny one—in their new kingdom.

Once here, they set about improving it. The old houses and temples were pulled down and splendid new ones erected in their stead. They designed a magnificent palace for themselves and Draupadi, and when they had entirely transformed the puny town into a prosperous city, fit for gods or emperors, they moved on to the next populated district and did the same there, until, in a very few years, the whole of the habitable part of their territory was more prosperous than any other part of India. On returning from this journey to their capital, which they had named

Indraprastha, the Pandavi decided to hold a coronation festival for their eldest brother, and a hundred messengers were soon despatched to summon neighbouring kings to the ceremony. It was well known that Duryodhana was their enemy, but courtesy demanded that he should be invited, and out of curiosity he accepted. His anger and jealousy knew no bounds when he beheld the wonderful city of Indraprastha, and the palace in its midst, and his ill-feeling was heightened when he mistook a crystal floor in one of the rooms for water, and lifted his robes to wade. He discovered his error directly, but the laughter of his companions mortified his pride. The next day he went into a room, in the centre of which was a pellucid pond, and mistaking this for ornamental crystal, he fell in. Soon afterwards he failed to see a doorway made of glass, and broke it by trying to walk through it. All this wrought him to an unendurable pitch of malice, and he returned to Hastinapura at the end of the festival, choking with spite and plans for vengeance.

Now, he knew that Yudhishthira had one great weakness. He was sure and strong in all points but one—he could not gamble except with the most disastrous results. If he tossed the dice but for five minutes, he lost all sense of fitness, all control ; the blood rushed to his brain, and like a madman he would stake, always to lose. Yudhishthira, knowing his own insufficiency, always refrained from the gambling table, and his friends, out of consideration, never challenged him ; for it is a knightly rule that a man, if challenged either to play or fight, must always face his challenger.

So it came into Duryodhana's crafty heart that through this weakness he would strike down his cousin, and without delay he sent an invitation to the Pandavi to attend a festive gathering at Hastinapura. When they arrived at their cousin's palace, they were fed and washed, and then led into the pleasure gardens, where, in many flower-bedecked pavilions, the tables had been set up. Duryodhana greeted his guests with apparent cordiality. "See," he said, "dicing is the order of the day. I challenge you, Yudhishthira, to a match." The Prince blanched, knowing himself to be entrapped. "Prithee, cousin, let one of my brothers play for me," he said. "Art afraid of my challenge, then ? " asked the other insolently. And the Prince, unable to refuse downright, cast a look of anguish towards his brethren, sent up a prayer to the Gods and began to play. The courtiers crowded round, jesting and laughing, betting on the likely losses and gains of the combatants; but the four Pandavi held themselves a little apart, knowing all too well what would be the upshot of the day's business.

Yudhishthira threw and lost. His face became pale, his hands trembled; he doubled the stakes and shouted " Again," like one in frenzy. For the second time he threw and lost. And the stakes again were doubled.

The watchers became silent as hour by hour passed, and the gamblers played for still

higher sums, till at length Yudhishthira had lost the whole of his treasury. The Pandavi were, in good sooth this time, beggars. But still he did not, or could not, stop. "My palace!" he cried, and when that had gone, "My country! My brothers! Myself!" And all were lost. The Pandavi were slaves.

"What is left? What is left?" screamed the intoxicated man.

"Draupadi, thy wife, is left," answered Duryodhana.

"Yes, yes; then I stake her too!"

The die was cast; and the Kuru Prince, with a cry of triumph, stood back from the table.

"Ha, ha!" he laughed. "Again am I the winner! The Gods be praised! And since you are now my slaves, and all your goods and treasures mine, you shall know the truth—that, from the days of our youth, Duryodhana has hated the Pandavi, and sworn to avenge unnumbered slights. This is his revenge; this is his triumph; and this is his decree. The Pandavi shall depart into the forest wildernesses, and there dwell for the space of thirteen years. Draupadi, their Queen, whom also I have won, shall become my slave, and shall sweep up the dust from the paths wherever I walk."

"Never, proud Prince," said a woman's voice ; and Draupadi herself, gloriously robed and attended, slowly made her way from the entrance of the pavilion to where Duryodhana and the Pandavi stood. She had learned from the auguries that an ill destiny awaited her husband in Hastinapura, and had hastened after him to warn and assist him, if she could. "Speak, my lords," she cried, looking from one

to another of the dumbfounded faces before her. " What has befallen ? "

So Arjuna told her, in broken words, of the fate that the gambler had brought upon them all ; and how she, too, had been staked and lost. A smile spread over her features, and she turned to the assembly, speaking in a clear, calm voice :

" Tell me, good sirs, can a slave sell or buy a free man ? "

" No, no," came the answer ; and then, addressing Duryodhana, she continued :

" Then neither can a man who has first lost himself, stake the freedom of a woman, even though she be his wife. Not until the earth dissolves shall the Queen of Yudhishthira bow the knee to the Kurus. If my lord and brethren must depart to the wilderness for thirteen years, then shall I go with them, and, the exile being over, the Pandavi shall return, and seek a fierce revenge."

At these stirring words, the lords and courtiers broke into applause, for though they feared, they hated, the Kuru Prince, and loved the five heroes who had now, by trickery as they could see, been robbed and exiled. Duryodhana flushed angrily, and bit his lip ; but he could not contradict the argument of the Princess, nor could he fail to be conscious of the anger his words and actions had aroused.

" Go, then," he cried ; " accompany your lord into beggary and misery. Perchance thirteen years among the hermits will cool your pride, even as it will wither your beauty and kill your youth ! "

And, with a mocking laugh, he turned on his heel and strode out of the pavilion.

Sadly then did the Pandavi and their Princess bid farewell to their friends, and much was the sorrow and many the tears that accompanied them on their way towards the forest.

As Yudhishthira reached the city gates, he turned, and held his hands high above his head as though invoking the curses of heaven upon Hastinapura.

Old Bhishma, too feeble now to arrest or control the course of events, saw the action, and, turning sadly to Dristarastra, spoke :

" The feud, my son, is now so hot that scarcely shall the tears of all the Gods quench it. In dust and ashes let us live through these thirteen years, for, when they are over, the Pandavi will surely return to smite and to kill. Thus only shall the breach between them and the Kurus be healed. What think you now of your eldest-born,

6

Duryodhana, who has been even as a weapon to smite asunder the interlaced branches of our house ?"

But Dristarastra said nothing, knowing in his heart that he had helped his son in his evil quarrel.

And as the Pandavi passed through the gates of Hastinapura, a peal of thunder shook the city to its foundations, and a blackness like night blotted out the sun.

PART IV
THE GREAT BATTLE

THIRTEEN weary years passed by, and at length the five champions and their Queen had paid the debt they owed to Duryodhana. On the first day of the fourteenth year, they emerged from hiding, and sought the capital of Drupada, in the land of Panchala. They knew that, for the sake of his daughter, he would be ready to lend them money and men, and that he would support them until such time as their plans for winning back their rights could be formed.

And Drupada did not fail them. He sent horsemen through the length and breadth of the country to summon to the capital all such as believed in the righteousness of the Pandava cause, and thousands of princes, knights, and peasants flocked to fight under the banners of the famous heroes.

News of these preparations reached Hastina-pura, and Duryodhana hastened to take counsel with Karna as to the best methods of meeting the threatened attack.

" I have not wasted these thirteen years in idleness as you, O Karna, know full well," he said. " I have made treaties with my neighbours, formed friendships, healed old enmities ; I have put aside the influence of Bhishma, and the policy of the court is not his, but mine ; my forces are strong, and I hold the capital. If only you will undertake the command of the army, I have no fear for the results."

But Karna, closely as he had attached himself to the Prince, shook his head, saying : " I cannot slay Yudhishthira and his brothers, and without their deaths your victory would not be complete. Against Arjuna only it is my desire to fight in single combat." And though Duryodhana pressed him for his reasons, he could gain no further confidence from him ; nevertheless, he promised at last to lead the battle, so strongly did Duryodhana urge him.

Now the story of Karna, ever surrounded by melancholy and mystery, was this.

His mother was actually no other than Kunti, the queen-parent of the five Pandavi. Before she married Pandu, their father, she had secretly been the wife of the Sun-god, and their child was Karna.

Kunti had prayed that if the Sun-god looked

with favour upon their offspring, he should bestow upon him a skin of metal—in fact, a " natural " suit of armour. In addition to this, she begged that to the child's ears should be fastened earrings, not to be severed from him except by cutting. And these things should be both a protection from earthly foes, and a sign of his immortality.

When the child was born, Kunti was overjoyed to see that her wish had been fulfilled ; but imagine her distress when, a few days later, a celestial messenger visited her at dead of night, and told her that the Sun desired her to put the child into a wicker basket on the morrow, and float it out on a current of the river Ganges without delay.

Kunti dared not disobey the will of heaven, but she never ceased to mourn the loss of her immortal babe.

She did not know how the waves carried him safely as far as the city of Champa, and that there an honest charioteer, by name Adiratha, and his wife found the child and nurtured him as though he had been their own ; until, at ripe age, he left his humble home, led by divine instinct, and sought the groves where Drona taught his noble pupils.

Now it was believed among the Gods that

destiny had willed Karna and Arjuna to be
mortal foes; and the God Indra, who had ever
looked with special favour upon Arjuna, loving
him with the love of a father, decided that, for
the sake of his favourite, the magical armour and
earrings, which rendered Karna invincible, must
somehow be stolen from him.

So one morning when Karna was praying at the
river-side, just after his bathe, Indra, in the guise
of a holy priest, approached him. He knew of
the lad's solemn vow, never to refuse a boon asked
by any Brahman at that sacred hour; so upon
the conclusion of the prayer, he cried in a feigned
voice: " A boon, a boon, sir ! "

" Ask," said Karna.

" Your mail and earrings, sir ! "

" Nay, I cannot give you those.　They are part of my body, and cannot be removed except by cutting."

" Cut, then, good sir, or else be it known in heaven and on earth that Karna cannot keep his vows."

At that moment, the Sun-god revealed to the boy the presence of Indra beneath the priestly garb.

" Aha ! " he exclaimed. "Is it thou, Indra, who dost demand my mail ? Since a God demands it, I cannot withhold it ; but thou shalt give me something in exchange."

"Gladly," answered Indra ; "what wilt thou ? "

"An arrow, that if it touches, kills," replied Karna. And the God gave him such an arrow, and took from him his skin of armour and his natural earrings; and, pleased with the success of his mission, ascended to the clouds.

From the moment that Karna had appeared among Drona's pupils, Kunti of course had secretly known who he was; and her grief overwhelmed her when one day she perceived that he had parted with the marks of his invincibility and immortality. However, she breathed no word of her distress to man or woman, trusting that the Sun-god, his father, would still protect him from harm; and the years rolled past, and Karna's position at Duryodhana's court strengthened, and Kunti, now grey-haired, rejoiced in his success, even though she saddened at the fortunes of her five other sons.

When she learned that the exiles had returned, and that war was imminent, it appeared horrible to her that Karna should lead the Kuru faction against his own half-brothers; and she determined to seek him at his hour of prayer, and tell him the truth at last.

As soon as Karna saw her, he saluted her humbly. "What is your will with me, lady-Queen?" he asked. "Am I not Karna, son of a charioteer, and friend of Duryodhana, whom, methinks, you have little cause to love?"

The Queen laid her hands upon his, and in trembling tones began to tell him that she indeed was his mother, and that his father was not a charioteer, but the bright and burning Sun. Before she had got far in her story, Karna smiled gently, and interrupted her.

"All this, Mother, I know. It was revealed to me many years ago in a dream. What is your will?"

"That you desert the faction of the Kurus, and, if you needs must fight, that you fight with your brethren the Pandavi, and not against them." At her words a ray of sunlight seemed to harden before their eyes, and a message in golden syllables rang down it. "Listen, O Karna, to the words of thy mother."

But Karna, casting his eyes up to the great orb above, solemnly addressed it.

"Not for either father or mother may I break the oath of fealty to Duryodhana. Nevertheless, I vow to injure none of my brothers, excepting only Arjuna, and him will I fight in single combat."

With this promise Kunti had to be satisfied, but many were the grief-worn nights she spent, waiting for the rival armies to descend to the plain where the conflict should take place.

After indescribable preparations, the Pandavi host at length emerged from Panchala, and swept like locusts towards Hastinapura ; but long before they came in sight of the city they saw Duryodhana's forces drawn up on the great plain of Kurushetra.

The opposing hosts shocked together, and, from that moment, for sixteen days they swayed to and fro in each other's grip, like wild animals let loose upon one another. Chariots were interlocked, and the drivers of them struggled madly to get free ; elephants trampled men, horses, and cars beneath their ponderous feet, and tore each other with their tusks ; banners floated for a moment, and then were dragged down, and ravelled to pieces ; arrows flew in showers, swords and scimitars flashed and whirled.

Only when night came on, always did the weary hosts retire, each to his own camp. The noise, the shouts, the groaning ceased ; and the moon and stars looked down upon thousands of war-stained heroes, all sleeping on the earth as peacefully as little children. But with the dawn the havoc began again, and no definite advantage came to either side.

On the seventeenth morning Karna awoke from a dream. He sought Duryodhana and told him that this was to be the day of destiny, and that before nightfall either he or Arjuna would have passed from the strife to rest in the lap of the Gods.

So saying, he went forth from the tents, and, conscious that the invincible arrow was safe in his quiver, he sought up and down the lines for his enemy.

At length they met ; and then began a conflict so terrible, yet wonderful, that the armies on either side ceased fighting to watch it ; and it was said afterwards by many, that they saw the figures of Gods pendent in the air, directing the weapons of the combatants.

The arrows of Arjuna surrounded Karna like a flock of birds, but ere they struck him, he bent his head, and they passed beyond their mark. Then, in his turn, he winged a shaft which sang, as it flew towards its enemy's heart ; but Arjuna sent one to meet it and deflected its course.

The rival archers were playing their last game ; sooner or later one must flag or fall ; one must send a dart that could be neither evaded nor repulsed.

" I must use the magic gift of Indra," at length thought Karna, for he perceived that his eyes were becoming dim, and his hand unsteady ; so he drew it from the quiver, and taking an aim that could not miss, he loosed it. But Indra had been guarding his favourite. Unseen by any, he pressed his foot upon the wheel of Arjuna's car, so that it sank a cubit into the earth, and the arrow carried away the Prince's diadem, but left his forehead unscathed.

Such was the spirit within the weapon, however, that having missed its aim, it returned of itself to the sender's hand, and whispered to him :

" Shoot again. This time I will follow his head howsoever he bends or turns it."

But Karna was too noble of mind to take advantage of arts not within the reach of his rival, and he cast the magic weapon down, saying :

" Karna never uses the same dart twice."

Arjuna, knowing nothing of what was passing in his enemy's mind—of how, because of honour, he was refusing an advantage—at that moment sped his strongest arrow, and cut Karna's head clean from his body.

Thus fell a hero of noble blood, killed in ignorance by his own half-brother ; for the cause of another he fell, and for the sake of an oath of fealty. The Sun hid his beams behind a cloud, the rivers ceased to sing, the snow melted upon the mountain-tops, the winds wailed ; when

Karna, the ill-fated son of Kunti, fell in the midst of the battle.

The Kurus wailed in token of defeat, the Pandavis sent up a shout of victory that tore the skies; and turning upon their enemies who fled in despair before them, the conquerors pursued them into their own territory.

It was with sad hearts that the five brethren approached the royal palace, for they knew that blind Dristarastra, his wife Gandhari, Kunti, Vidura, and many another aged kinsman, were waiting for the news ; and they dreaded telling them of the carnage in which so many of the flower of the land had perished.

But when they heard, they did not wail or moan. " It is the will of heaven," said Dristarastra, " and a just punishment upon my house for our long enmity to the Pandavi. Little is left me now in this world. I will go, therefore, to the banks of the Ganges, and there my life shall flicker out its short length, while I devote my heart to piety and prayer."

Gandhari, his wife, wished to accompany him ; and the Pandavi decided that they, too, would sojourn for a month with their uncle beside the sacred waters, and here, in quiet meditation, aloof from the world, would form their plans for ruling, with equity and kindness, the kingdom which, after so many years of hardship, they had finally inherited. And so well did they make these plans, and so excellently carried them out afterwards, that there went a saying over all India :

" As soldiers the Pandavi are heroes, but as Kings they are almost Gods."

THE FLUTE-PLAYER

WHEN Prince Vasudev married Princess Devaki, Kans, the King of Mathura, was the only man who did not rejoice at the splendid wedding ceremony. Although he had given his consent to the royal marriage and had approved of his sister Devaki's choice of a husband, the king's heart was full of gloom and foreboding. Early that morning he had been visited by a soothsayer, who warned him that his death would result from this marriage.

" I have read in the stars that the first-born son of Devaki shall slay his kingly uncle," the soothsayer declared solemnly. More than this he could not tell the king, and, as it was too late to prevent the wedding, Kans had to conceal his disapproval. So he sat at the feast eating and drinking sparingly, pondering all the time over the strange words of the soothsayer and planning how to protect himself in the future.

Now Vasudev and Devaki loved each other dearly, and, unaware of the emnity of Kans, they lived happily in Mathura for a while. By and by a son was born to them, a singularly beautiful child whom they called Krishna. On the day of his birth there were signs and portents that the gods themselves rejoiced at the event, for although it was but early in the spring the small buds on the trees burst into full leaf, fragrant flowers unfolded their petals, and the birds sang with celestial beauty of sound.

Kans heard of the child's birth with fear and anger. He sent messages of congratulation to Vasudev and Devaki, then taking one of his courtiers aside he bade him find means whereby the infant should be destroyed secretly.

The courtier was ashamed to take part in such an infamous plot, so he hastened to Vasudev: "Guard your child well, O Prince!" he said, "for the king is evilly disposed towards him."

He would say no more in answer to Vasudev's horrified questioning, so the prince consulted his wife as to what they should do.

"We must say that the child is dead," said Devaki, "and to-night you must bear him away to some safe place far from Mathura. Better we should part with him than to leave him in danger here."

So that night Vasudev disguised himself and slipped away with his precious burden, and it was reported the next day that little Krishna had died in his sleep. Vasudev travelled in haste to Gokula, a pleasant spot many, many leagues away, where he found a worthy childless couple called Nand and Yasoda. Telling them of his difficulties, he besought them to take charge of the infant, and the good people promised to bring up Krishna as if he were their own son.

Vasudev then returned to Mathura; but before many days had passed Kans, upon some slight pretext, ordered him and Devaki to be imprisoned, and the unhappy pair languished in a grim fortress, while Kans, believing Krishna to be dead, reigned with a feeling of security for many years.

Meanwhile little Krishna grew vigorous and handsome. Every one in Gokula was charmed with him, and although he was a very mischievous little boy people forgave him his pranks on account of the love they bore him. One day when he had been particularly naughty his kind foster-mother sighed and shook her head.

"O Krishna!" she said, "what would your real father and mother do with such a mischievous son?"

"Are you and Nand not my real parents, then?" asked the boy.

Yasoda told him the truth—how on account of his wicked uncle he had been banished from

7

Mathura, and Krishna, throwing his arms around her, cried: " I will be good, and when I am a man I will seek this Kans and slay him ! "

From that day Krishna was full of gratitude towards his foster-parents, and, as they were humble folk, as soon as he was old enough to help them he became a cow-herd. He enjoyed his life amongst the herd-boys and soon became their leader. Amongst his many accomplishments he could play the flute so beautifully that the birds ceased to sing and perched motionless upon the boughs to listen to him, and wild animals grew tame and forbore to attack him when he played. And every maiden who heard the wordless songs of Krishna fell in love with him ; but as yet he cared for none of them.

Now, it happened that the same soothsayer who had visited Mathura long ago returned to the kingdom and Kans consulted him again. To the king's amazement the soothsayer repeated the old prophecy : " The first-born son of Devaki shall slay his kingly uncle."

The king realised that he must have been tricked, and his fury was unbounded. He happened to know of a magician living not far from Mathura, so he went to him in secret and promised to reward him well if the old man would find some means of slaying Krishna. The magician promised the king that this evil deed should be performed, and Kans waited impatiently for news of his nephew's death.

One morning, soon afterwards, Krishna and his friends the herd-boys led their cattle to the brink of a stream, and after the first cow had drunk some of the water it fell dead on the bank.

" The stream must be poisoned ! " cried Krishna, and, as he leaned over the water wondering what deadliness was lurking within, a snake wound itself around his body and strove to strike him a blow with its fiery fang. Krishna, with supernatural strength, flung the snake from him and stamped upon its head.

Kans, having waited some time for news, again visited the magician, and hearing that the poisonous snake had failed to destroy Krishna besought the old man to devise more evil. The magician now sent a fierce elephant to Gokula. Meeting Krishna alone in a forest, the animal rushed at him, but he played upon his flute with such sweetness that the elephant stood still to listen to him, and Krishna managed to make his escape unharmed.

Now, the strength and valour of Krishna and the charm of his music began to be famous far and wide, and a certain beautiful princess called Rukmini heard of these things, and, although she had never seen Krishna, she felt that he was the only man she could love in all the world. So when her father told her it was time that she chose a husband she answered : " My mind is set upon Krishna the cow-herd."

Her father laughed scornfully, and said : " Shall a princess wed such a base-born creature ? Nay, my daughter, the King of Chanderi has asked for your hand in marriage and it is he whom you shall accept."

Rukmini was terrified at the prospect, so she contrived to send a letter to Krishna begging him to rescue a luckless princess from an unhappy marriage.

Krishna, who was always ready to rescue those in distress, hastened to the palace where Rukmini dwelt and learned that her father had carried out his threat : she was to be married to the King of Chanderi on the following day. Krishna waited until night-time ; then, having discovered the position of Rukmini's sleeping apartment, he stood outside one of the windows and played very softly upon his flute. Rukmini, who was lying sleepless, crept to the window and saw the dim figure of the flute-player. Then Krishna climbed the wall, seized the princess in his arms, and contrived to bear her away in the darkness.

Together they fled to Gokula, and when Krishna beheld the gentle beauty of Rukmini his heart was touched for the first time, but he feared to tell her of his love because of his lowly calling. Then Rukmini told him how she had fallen in love with him even before they had met and that gladly would she exchange the grandeur of her life in a palace for the simple existence of a cow-herd's wife. So the two lovers were wed, and they lived happily in Gokula until Krishna decided that it was time for him to visit his real parents. Taking tender leave of Nand and Yasoda, Krishna and Rukmini journeyed to Mathura, where they found the chief city hung with flags and garlands, for a great tournament was about to take place.

The tournament had been ordered by Kans, who had already obtained news of Krishna's proposed visit to Mathura. The king's wrestlers were famous throughout India, and the wily Kans hoped that Krishna would enter the lists and surely be overcome.

It happened, at the beginning, as Kans had foreseen. Krishna, who was proud of his prowess as a wrestler, challenged one of the king's men ; a long and arduous combat took place, ending in victory for Krishna.   A second wrestler appeared, then a third, and even a fourth, and each time Krishna defeated his opponent. At last Kans, who was watching, grew desperate, and while Krishna was resting before his fifth combat the king came behind him and was about to plunge a knife into his shoulder, when Krishna turned, seized Kans by the throat, and killed him with his powerful hands.

Then he revealed himself to the populace as Krishna the son of Devaki, and told his story, and the people acclaimed him as a hero. He learned with horror of the imprisonment of his parents and rushed to free them from the fortress. Great was the rejoicing of Vasudev and Devaki over their new-found son, who, now that Kans was dead, was heir to the throne of Mathura.

Thenceforward Krishna reigned wisely over his people and was known as a champion of the oppressed, for he was ever ready to use his strength and power in defeating the wicked.

THE HARD-HEARTED PRINCESS

THERE was once a young Prince named Kusa who was famed for his benevolence and wisdom, but unfortunately he was extremely ugly. It is true

103

there was no one in the kingdom who liked him less on that account, but poor Kusa was very sensitive about his ill-favoured appearance, and whenever his father, King Okkaka, urged him to marry, he would answer sadly—

" Never ask me to wed, for how could a beautiful maiden love such an ugly fellow as I am ? "

Now, King Okkaka was never satisfied with this reply, and at last Kusa grew so weary of refusing to choose a bride, that he devised a scheme whereby he hoped to free himself for ever from this vexing question of his marriage. Therefore he fashioned a golden image, and when he showed the King his handiwork, he said firmly—

" If a maiden as beautiful as this image be found for me, I will make her my bride ; otherwise I will remain unwed."

Kusa felt quite safe in making this promise, for, as the statue which he had wrought was fairer than the Goddess of Beauty herself, he thought that no mortal maiden would ever be found who could compare favourably with his golden image. However, King Okkaka by no means despaired of being able to discover such a peerless beauty, and he commanded certain messengers to travel far and wide in search of this exquisite maiden.

The messengers visited many lands, bearing the statue with them ; and every time they arrived at a city or a village, they inquired whether the inhabitants knew of any maiden who resembled the golden image. But nowhere was such a beauty to be found until the travellers reached the kingdom of Madda.

Now it happened that the King of Madda had eight lovely daughters, and the eldest of them, whose name was Pabhavati, was not only reputed to be the fairest maiden in the world, but she was extraordinarily like the golden image ; indeed, Kusa might have fashioned it from her living self ! When the messengers had convinced themselves of this wonderful resemblance, they begged audience with the King of Madda, and informed his Majesty that they had come to ask the hand of the Princess Pabhavati for noble Prince Kusa, the son of King Okkaka.

The King of Madda had heard many things concerning the power of King Okkaka, so he replied graciously—

" If your Royal master will come hither with a great retinue, I will give him the hand of Princess Pabhavati for his son, Prince Kusa."

The messengers hastened to King Okkaka with their good tidings, and the King was delighted at the success of their mission, but poor Kusa's heart was filled with dismay.

" Alas ! my Father," he cried mournfully to the King, " how will such a beautiful Princess behave when she sees how hideous I am ? She will surely flee from me at once."

" Have no fear, my son," answered King Okkaka, " for I will revive an ancient custom of our family to protect you. This custom decrees that a bride shall not look upon the face of her husband until one year after her marriage. Therefore, for one whole year, you must only meet your bride in a darkened apartment."

" But how will such a thing avail me in the end ? " asked Kusa doubtfully. " I shall still be ugly when the Princess beholds me."

" That will not matter," replied the King ; " for, during that year, your bride will have learned to love you so much that, when she looks upon you at last, you will not be ugly in her eyes."

Kusa was still unconvinced as to the wisdom of this marriage, but King Okkaka insisted upon travelling to the land of Madda without delay, and before long he returned in triumph with the beautiful Princess Pabhavati.

However much he feared the consequences, the Prince was now obliged to fulfil his promise to wed, so the marriage ceremony was performed in a darkened apartment, by command of the King.

Princess Pabhavati was astonished to learn that she must not look upon the face of her husband for one year after the marriage had taken place.

" To what strange land has my father sent me ? " she thought wonderingly, but she expressed not a word of disapproval at this family custom, and allowed herself to be installed in a magnificent suite of apartments, one room of which was always to be kept in utter darkness.

To this mysterious chamber, therefore, Kusa came daily to visit his bride, and since his voice and manners were kind and gentle, and he was wondrously skilled as a musician, Pabhavati soon grew to love him, although she never caught a glimpse of his face. He spent many hours in playing to her upon his lute, or telling her thrilling stories of adventure, and she would listen to him, enraptured, thinking all the while—

" Was there ever a Prince before like this husband of mine ? How I long for the day when I shall behold his face ! Surely he will be as handsome and noble-looking as he is good and wise."

Now, all might have been well if Pabhavati had been contented to wait for a year until she saw

Kusa, but, after she had been married for one month only, the Princess began to wonder more and more what her husband was really like. At the end of the second month she could not conceal her curiosity, and, when Kusa was with her in the darkened room one day, she said coaxingly—

"Dear husband, it grieves me sorely that I must wait so many months before I may look upon your face. I beseech you to meet me in the light of day."

"Nay, my Pabhavati, such a thing is impossible," answered the Prince in alarm. "I cannot disobey the decree of my father the King. Have patience, I implore you. The months of waiting will pass only too quickly."

But patience was the very thing the Princess lacked the most, and she now began to question her waiting-women concerning her husband's appearance. The evasive answers which she received only served to heighten her curiosity, so at last she bribed one of her attendants to help her obtain a glimpse of Kusa in secret.

On a certain day, therefore, when this waiting-woman knew that the Prince was to ride through the city, she concealed the Princess in an upper apartment of the palace, a window of which looked upon the broad highway.

In breathless suspense Pabhavati waited for her husband to appear. Presently she heard the sound of music and joyous shouting, and the procession came slowly through the city street, past the windows of the great white palace.

"Long live Kusa, our noble Prince," cried the mob, waving gay banners and strewing garlands at the feet of the white elephant upon which Kusa was riding in state.

Pabhavati stared eagerly beneath the great umbrella which was shading the prince from the glare of the sun, then she shrank back with a look of horror upon her lovely face.

" What ! " she cried. " Can that hideous creature be my husband ? Nay, that is not my Kusa."

The waiting-woman assured her that she had indeed beheld the Prince, whereupon Pabhavati declared that she would flee instantly from such an ugly husband. So she angrily demanded that an escort should be given her to the land of Madda, for she considered that she was no longer bound by marriage to a Prince who was so different from what she had fondly imagined.

King Okkaka would have forced the scornful Princess to remain in the palace, but Kusa said sorrowfully—

" Nay, let her have her will."

Then, forgetful of all the love and tenderness which Kusa had lavished upon her, and thinking only of his poor ugly face, Pabhavati was driven away, and the Prince felt as if she had taken all the joy and happiness in the world with her.

For a time he was inconsolable, but one day the thought occurred to him that if he were to seek Pabhavati in her own land, he might find that she had grown more kindly disposed towards him. This idea had no sooner flashed through his mind than he proceeded to act upon it. He changed his princely robes for simple garments, and, taking his lute, he set out on foot for the kingdom of Madda.

After he had journeyed for many days and slept for many nights beneath the stars, Kusa arrived one evening at the land of Madda, and he hastened onward to the chief city wherein Pabhavati dwelt.

It was midnight when he reached the Royal palace, and he crept beneath the walls and played upon his lute those soft melodies with which he had once charmed the ears of his Princess. The sleepers in the palace stirred and smiled in their slumbers, for they dreamed that they were listening to celestial music, but Pabhavati wakened with a start and sat upright upon her couch.

" That is Kusa beneath my window," she thought,

with mingled fear and anger. " If my father should learn that he has come hither, surely I shall be forced to return to this ugly Prince. What shall I do ? "

But Kusa had no intention of appealing to the King of Madda, for unless Pabhavati should come back to him of her own free will, he felt that he would rather lose her for ever. Therefore he determined to keep the tidings of his arrival in the city a secret from every one excepting the Princess.

" I will send some token to the palace which Pabhavati alone will recognise," he thought hopefully, and when morning came he sought the chief potter in the city and asked to become his apprentice.

" If I work well for you, will you display my wares in the palace of the King ? " asked Kusa.

" Certainly, if they be worthy of such an honour," answered the potter. " Show me what you can do."

Kusa sat down at the potter's wheel, and the clay specimens he produced were so beautifully formed that his new master cried gleefully : " Surely the King will purchase these dainty wares for his daughters ; " and he carried some of the bowls which Kusa had made straightway to the palace.

The King was enchanted with the potter's new wares, and, when he learned that they had been fashioned by a young apprentice, his Majesty cried : " Give the youth a thousand golden pieces, and tell him that henceforward he must work only for my daughters. Now carry eight of these beautiful bowls to the Princesses as my gifts to them this day."

The potter did as he was commanded, and the King's daughters marvelled at the beauty of

8

their father's gifts; but Pabhavati caught sight of her own likeness imprinted upon the bowls, and she felt certain that they had been wrought by Kusa. So she flung her gift aside and said scornfully to the potter—

"Take this ugly bowl back to your apprentice and tell him that I will have none of his work."

Kusa sighed deeply when the potter told him what the Princess Pabhavati had said.

"Alas! she still despises me for my ugliness," he said to himself. "If I could speak with her, perchance I might be able to touch her hard heart. I will take service in the palace to be near her."

So he gave the potter the King's gold pieces and bade him farewell; then he presented himself at the Royal kitchens where he heard that the chief cook was in need of an apprentice.

The cook allowed Kusa to enter his service at once, and the Prince proved himself to be so extraordinarily skilful, that a dish prepared by him alone was sent straightway to the King.

His Majesty partook of this dish with much enjoyment, and, when he heard that the delicious food had been cooked by a new apprentice, he cried: "Give him a thousand pieces of gold, and henceforward let him prepare and serve all the food for myself and my daughters."

PABHAVATI WAKENED WITH A START
From "The Hard-hearted Princess"

Kusa joyfully gave the King's gold pieces to the chief cook, and now set to work to prepare many delicious dishes.

To Pabhavati's dismay, therefore, she presently beheld her husband, in the guise of a cook, staggering into her apartment with a heavy load of dishes. As he made no sign of recognition, she grew bold, and, staring scornfully at his mournful countenance, she said with a proud air : " I care not for these dishes. Bring me food that other hands than yours have prepared."

Her sisters cried out that she was indeed foolish, for never before had they tasted such delicious cooking. But although Kusa came day after day laden with fresh dainties, Pabhavati would never touch a single dish that he had prepared.

At last the poor Prince felt that he was powerless to soften the heart of his cruel Princess.

" Nothing I can do will please her," he thought bitterly. " For weeks I have endured hardships in order to be near her, and to serve her, now I will leave her for ever. I will return to my father, and perchance I may find some hermitage in the kingdom wherein I may hide my loneliness and sorrow."

But while he was preparing to leave the palace, Kusa heard that the King of Madda was sorely troubled. Tidings had been brought to his Majesty that seven monarchs were riding towards the city with seven armies, and that each of these monarchs, having heard of the beauty of Pabhavati, was desirous of making her his wife.

The King was most perplexed by the difficulties of his position, for he felt sure that if he selected *one* of these suitors as the husband of Pabhavati, the other six would wage war upon the kingdom of Madda out of revenge.

" If only Pabhavati had never left her rightful husband," thought the King, " these troubles would not have arisen."

However, it was useless to spend his time in regretting the past, so the King sent for some wise men and asked them which suitor he had better choose for the Princess.

" Not one of them alone," declared the wise men solemnly. " The Princess has endangered the peace of the realm, therefore she must suffer the consequences of her fatal attraction. She must be slain, her body divided into seven pieces, and one portion presented to each of the seven monarchs. In this manner only can disastrous wars be avoided."

The King was horror-stricken at this ghastly

advice, and, when the wise men had left his presence, he sat alone deep in troubled thought.

Suddenly Kusa, still in his cook's attire, appeared before him and said—

" I pray your Majesty, let me deal with these monarchs. Give me an army and I will subdue these suitors or perish in the attempt."

" What!" cried his Majesty in astonishment. " Shall a servant do battle with kings ? "

" I am no servant, but that unhappy Kusa, to whom you did once entrust your daughter," answered the Prince. " Therefore it is fitting that I should deal with these suitors, I alone."

The King could not believe that it was Kusa who stood before him. He summoned Pabhavati to his presence, and when the Princess admitted that this cook's apprentice was really her husband, he cried, "Shame upon you, my daughter, for allowing your husband to be treated as a menial in the palace."

Then he dismissed Pabhavati with angry words, and begged Kusa's pardon for the slights which had been offered him.

Kusa declared that the only reparation he required was the power to deal with the seven monarchs, so the King immediately placed him at the head of an army and gave him leave to act as he thought best.

The seven monarchs were astonished when they saw Kusa and his forces riding towards them, but their surprise quickly turned to dismay, for, in spite of their superior numbers, they were soon utterly routed by their brave enemy. Therefore they were obliged to lay down their arms and surrender themselves to Kusa, who led them as captives to the King of Madda.

" Deal with these prisoners as you will, O King," cried the triumphant Prince; but the King replied—

" Nay, brave Kusa, they are your captives. It is for you to decide their fate."

" Then," said the Prince, " since each of these

monarchs is desirous of wedding a beautiful Princess, why do you not marry them all to the sisters of Pabhavati ? ''

This suggestion was joyfully received by all who were concerned in the matter. The King felt that the safety of his kingdom would now be ensured for ever ; the seven monarchs were delighted at the beauty and grace of Pabhavati's sisters, while the Princesses themselves looked favourably upon the husbands who had been chosen for them.

Meanwhile, Pabhavati sat alone, weeping bitter tears, for she had begun to realise how heartlessly she had treated Kusa, and what a noble lover she had rejected.

" Alas ! he will never forgive me," she was thinking sadly, when a message was brought to her that Kusa was desirous of speech with her.

She hastened to the apartment where the Prince stood awaiting her, and, casting herself at his feet, she cried humbly : " Forgive me, oh my husband, and take me back, even though you treat me as a slave. Let me prove my repentance by serving you all my days."

Kusa gently raised her from the ground. " Do you wish to return to me ? " he asked sadly.

"Look at me, Pabhavati. I am still as ugly, alas! as when you fled from me."

Pabhavati gazed at him steadfastly, but instead of the loathing which poor Kusa had been wont to read in her eyes of late, he saw nothing but wonder and tenderness there now.

"Surely you are changed," she cried, "for to me you no longer appear ugly."

But it was Pabhavati who had altered. Instead of the ugliness of Kusa's appearance, she was now able to see his goodness, wisdom, and courage reflected upon his countenance, and henceforward she was a tender, loving wife to the husband she had once so cruelly scorned.

THE STORY OF THE WHITE ELEPHANT

IN far-off days, when animals possessed the gift of speech, there dwelt a great herd of elephants in a wooded region near the Himalaya Mountains. They were all handsome creatures, but the finest elephant in the tribe was a big white animal who had a truly noble nature.

Now, unfortunately, the mother of this white elephant was old and blind, and although her son gathered sweet wild fruits for her every day, he was often distressed to find that the other elephants had stolen the poor animal's food. He rebuked them many times for their thoughtless greed, but, as they still continued to rob his mother, he led her aside one day and said to her—

"Mother, it would be better if you and I were to dwell alone. Come with me to a distant cave which I have discovered."

The mother elephant raised no objection to this plan, so her son guided her steps to the cave, which was pleasantly situated near a glade of wild fruit trees and a little lake covered with lotus blooms. For a time the two elephants dwelt happily in this peaceful spot, until one evening, when they were resting in the cave, they heard loud cries echoing through the vast woods around them.

" Listen, Mother," said the white elephant. " Surely that is the voice of some human being in distress. I will hasten to see if I can be of service to him."

" Nay, do not go, my son," replied his mother solemnly. " I am old and blind, it is true, yet well do I know the ways of human beings towards our race. If you help this man, your goodness will be rewarded by treachery."

But the white elephant could not bear the thought of suffering, so he said gently—

" Forgive me, Mother, but I cannot listen unmoved to these cries," and he hurried away in the direction whence the shouting seemed to come. By the lotus lake he discovered a man dressed as a forester, and at the elephant's approach the terrified fellow tried to flee, but the good animal said kindly—

" Do not fear me, O stranger, but tell me what ails you. Perchance I can help you."

" Alas ! noble elephant," answered the distracted forester, " what can you do for me ? For seven days and nights I have been lost in this vast, uninhabited region. How shall I find my way back to Benares where my home is situated?"

"That is an easy matter," said the elephant joyfully; "for, if you will climb upon my back, I will bear you once more to the haunts of men."

The forester gladly did as he was told, and the elephant carried him swiftly through the great woods until they reached open country again.

"Yonder lies the city of Benares," said the elephant as the forester dismounted. "Nay, do not thank me, for I am proud to have rendered you a service."

Then, without a thought that evil could possibly result from his kind action, the elephant returned lightheartedly to his distant cave.

Unfortunately the forester was of a cunning and avaricious disposition, and, while he had been carried through the woods, instead of being grateful to his rescuer, he had been thinking—

"Before I left Benares the King's white elephant had just died. Surely his Majesty would reward me richly if I were to capture this fine animal for him."

So the treacherous forester had carefully noted certain trees and hills as landmarks upon his journey, and as soon as he reached the city of Benares once more, he craved audience of the King.

" Your Majesty," he cried eagerly, " I have seen the very animal to replace your deceased elephant ; " and he proceeded to describe his rescuer with such enthusiasm that the King said—

" Gladly would I possess such a fine creature. Go back to the forest with a band of my most skilful elephant trainers, and if they succeed in capturing this noble animal, you shall be well rewarded."

So the forester led the trainers back to the lotus lake without any difficulty, and they found the white elephant gathering fruits for his mother's evening meal. At the sound of footsteps, he turned his head, and when he beheld the forester with the band of trainers, the poor animal realised that he had been betrayed.

He tried to escape, but the trainers pursued him, and, by means of their great skill, they soon succeeded in capturing him ; then they led him through the forest towards the city of Benares in triumph.

Meanwhile the poor mother elephant was awaiting her son's return, and when night came and he was still absent, she bemoaned her fate, for she felt certain that he had been captured.

" Alas ! " she wailed. " What shall I do without my son ? Who will bring me sweet wild fruits or lead me to the lotus lake for water? I shall die of hunger and thirst in this lonely spot. Would that we had never left the herd."

But deep as her distress was, the heart of her son was heavier still, as his captors led him to Benares. "My poor mother!" he thought. "What will she do without me? If only I had listened to her advice concerning mankind I should still be free to cherish her. Now she will end her days in misery."

In spite of his dejected look, however, the elephant found favour in the eyes of the King, who declared that henceforward he would ride upon no other animal than this splendid white creature.

The forester and the trainers were richly rewarded for their fine capture, and the elephant was placed in the royal stable which had been richly decorated in his honour.

Now, a few days afterwards, the King wished to ride in state through the city, and he commanded that the white elephant should be prepared to carry him, but the trainers cried in great distress : " Your Majesty, the white elephant is ailing grievously, for he has refused to touch a morsel of food since he was brought into the city, although we have placed the choicest fruits and grasses before him." In great alarm the King hastened to the stable and when he saw the white elephant standing in an attitude of suffering and despair, he cried—

" O good animal, how you are changed ! Why do you refuse to eat ? Is it that you care not for the food which my trainers have provided for you ? " The elephant shook his great head mournfully in reply.

" Then speak," said the King eagerly. " Only tell me what you wish, and it shall be granted if possible."

" O great King," answered the elephant in feeble tones, " all I desire is to return to my poor blind mother in the forest, for while she is alone and starving there, how can I eat ? The thought of food is loathsome to me." Then the elephant told the King how he had been obliged to keep his mother apart from the herd, and how happily he had dwelt with her alone until the forester had ruined their peace by his treacherous act.

Now the King was just and benevolent, and, although he sorely coveted the white elephant for himself, he cried without hesitation—

" O noble animal, your goodness puts mankind to shame. I give you your freedom, so return to your mother and cherish her as tenderly as you have done hitherto."

After praising his Majesty, the elephant hastened from Benares as fast as his feeble limbs could carry him, and when he reached the cave once more, he found to his great joy that his mother was still alive. " Ah, my son," she said, when he was telling her the story of his capture, " you should have listened to me. Human beings are ever evilly disposed towards us."

" Not all of them, Mother," he cried triumphantly ; " for had the King not been noble and generous, I should still be in captivity. Let us forget the treachery of the forester and think only of the King's benevolence." And, from that time, that is just what the grateful elephants did.

SAKUNTALA, OR THE RING OF REMEMBRANCE

LONG, long ago, when men worshipped the great god Indra, there lived a young Indian King named Dushyanta, who was well beloved by his subjects.

Now it happened, one day, that whilst he was hunting in a vast forest, King Dushyanta became separated from his followers, and he wandered on amidst great trees and shrubs laden with blossom until he found himself in a pleasant grove which led to a hermitage. This secluded little dwelling was the abode of an old hermit called Father Kanva, and the king, who had heard many stories concerning the piety and wisdom of the holy man, determined to honour him with a visit this very day.

As Dushyanta drew near the hermitage, he was entranced by the peaceful beauty of his surroundings. The cool air was fragrant with the scent of jasmine flowers, the birds sang softly amidst the trees, and a stream bordered with lotus blooms flowed swiftly by the sacred dwelling.

To the King's regret, however, the hermitage

"MY FATHER IS ABSENT ON A PILGRIMAGE AND HAS LEFT
ME HERE TO WELCOME GUESTS"

was empty, and he was about to leave the grove in search of his followers when a gentle voice cried, " Wait, my lord," and a young girl appeared before him.

In spite of her coarse dress, which was made from the bark of a tree, the girl was so beautiful and noble-looking that the King's interest and admiration were aroused, and he asked her courteously : " Is not this hermitage the dwelling-place of holy Kanva ? "

" Yes, my lord," she replied ; " but my father is absent on a pilgrimage, and has left me here to welcome guests.   I pray you, rest a while."

She hastened to bring water and luscious fruits for his refreshment, and the King was delighted at her pleasant hospitality.   It was evident from her manner that she did not observe the exalted rank of her guest, so Dushyanta, who loved to mingle unrecognised with his people, pretended to be an ordinary huntsman, and asked the hermit girl her name in return.

" I am called Sakuntala," she said, and as the King begged her to tell him more about herself, she added that she was the adopted daughter of Father Kanva.

She had been left an orphan when she was a tiny child, but good Kanva had treated her as lovingly as if he had really been her father, and, though she was of noble birth, she was quite content to live this simple life amongst the sweet-throated birds and fragrant flowers of the forest.

As Dushyanta listened to her voice and watched her beautiful face, he felt that he could linger in this enchanting spot for ever, but he knew that his followers must be anxiously searching for him, so he took leave of Sakuntala and made his way back to the huntsmen.

He did not leave the forest, however, but ordered his men to encamp at some distance from the hermitage, and the next day, and the following day as well, found him in the grove with the gentle hermit girl.

Before long Dushyanta and Sakuntala were confessing their love for each other, but when the girl learned that it was the King himself, who wished to wed her, she was dismayed and protested that surely he would live to regret his rash choice.

However, Dushyanta managed to soothe her fears, and, dreading lest something might occur to separate him from her, he prevailed upon Sakuntala to wed him without delay.

There was no need for a priest to marry the lovers, since, in those days, it was lawful for great

Kings and warriors to wed their brides without ceremonies, so, in the shady grove where they had first met, Dushyanta and Sakuntala vowed to be true to each other for ever.

The King was so happy with his bride that he would gladly have spent his life alone with her in the forest, but he knew that duty recalled him to his subjects.

"Come with me to my palace, dear Sakuntala," he said tenderly. "You shall have costly jewels and garments of the finest texture, and my people shall acknowledge you as their Queen."

Now the only thing to mar Sakuntala's happiness was the fear that Father Kanva might be angry, when he came back from his pilgrimage, to find her wedded, so she answered: "Dear Husband, I cannot leave the forest until I have told

Father Kanva of our marriage. Also he left the hermitage in my charge, remember, and if I were to accompany you now, who could give hospitality to guests ? No, Dushyanta, you must return to your palace alone, but come back to me soon, I entreat you, for I shall then be ready to join you."

The King was very reluctant to leave his wife, but he saw clearly the wisdom of her remarks, so he placed a ring, engraven with the name " Dushyanta," upon her finger, and swore by the golden circlet that ere many days had passed he would return to the hermitage and claim his bride from Father Kanva.

The King departed, and Sakuntala felt that the days would seem endless until she saw him again.

She wandered disconsolately about the forest after he had gone, forgetting to be near the hermitage in case a guest should arrive, and when she came back to the grove at nightfall, to her dismay she was confronted by a visitor who was almost choking with anger.

The new-comer was an old sage named Durvasas, who was dreaded by all because of his violent temper, and it was said that if any one were unfortunate enough to offend him, he would punish them with unjust severity.

Durvasas had been waiting at the hermitage

for a long time, and he considered that he had been grievously slighted. In vain Sakuntala pleaded for forgiveness, and begged him to accept hospitality now ; but the old man was angered beyond control, and, thrusting the girl aside, he hurried away muttering a curse upon her under his breath.

Sakuntala was troubled to think she had neglected her duty, and she knew how serious an offence she had really committed, for it was looked upon as a great sin by the Indian people, if, by chance, a guest were to visit them and depart unhonoured from their dwelling.

However, something happened the next day which grieved her still more. Whilst she was bathing in the stream near at hand, her cherished ring, the king's gift, slipped from her finger and disappeared in the foaming waters.

Sakuntala wept bitterly at her loss, but she little knew what misery it was to bring her in the future, or how closely this misfortune was connected with the angry Durvasas.

It was a great relief to her, when Father Kanva returned from his pilgrimage, to find that he was not displeased at the tidings of her marriage ; on the contrary, the holy man seemed to be overjoyed at her story.

" My daughter, thou art worthy even of the great Dushyanta," he said tenderly. " Gladly will I give thee to the King when he shall arrive to claim thee," and Sakuntala wept happy tears, thinking that, except for the loss of her ring, she was the most favoured of mortals.

Days passed by and Sakuntala began to feel a weight at her heart, for the King neither came nor sent a messenger to her.

What could have happened ? she asked herself. Was Dushyanta ill, or had he repented of his rash choice ? Ah no, she could never believe that, yet why did he not come when she was so weary of longing for him ?

Then Father Kanva, too, grew uneasy, and he said : " My daughter, since the King doth not come, thou must seek him in his palace. Make ready for thy journey without delay, for though it grieveth me to part with thee, my beloved child, yet a wife should be at her husband's side."

Sakuntala did not know whether to rejoice at the thought of meeting Dushyanta or to dread this journey, which seemed like an act of disobedience to her husband. Had he not said, as he parted from her, " Wait for me here, my Sakuntala, I shall soon return ? " However, she could not refuse to do Father Kanva's bidding, so, for the first time in her life, she set out through the great forest to the unknown world beyond.

After many days she reached the royal city, and, learning that the King was in his palace, she begged admittance to his Majesty's presence, saying that she had brought tidings of great importance.

How fast her heart beat when she found herself at the foot of the King's throne, and through her heavy veil she could watch his beloved countenance !

" What is your will ? " Dushyanta asked kindly, and at the sound of his voice Sakuntala grew radiant with joy and hope.

" My lord," she answered, throwing back her veil, " do not be angry with me, but since you did not keep your promise to claim me soon, I have been forced to seek you here."

"My promise to claim you? What do you mean?" cried Dushyanta in a bewildered tone.

Sakuntala gazed at him with fear in her eyes.

"O Dushyanta, you are mocking me," she said sorrowfully. "Have you forgotten our wedding in the forest, how you vowed to cherish me for

ever ?   Do not look so strangely at me, I beseech
you, but acknowledge me as your bride, according
to your promise."

"My bride !" repeated the King.   "What story
is this ?   I have never seen you before."

Poor Sakuntala could hardly believe her own ears.

"What has happened to my lord ? " she
whispered to herself.   "I have always dreaded
lest he should repent of our hasty marriage, yet
surely he cannot mean to deny me."

Then she stretched out her arms appealingly to
Dushyanta, and cried—

"How can you say such words ? they are not
worthy of a king.   Alas ! what have I done that
you should treat me so cruelly ? "

"I have never seen you before," the King
protested firmly.   "Are you mad or wicked that
you should come to me with such an idle tale ? "

Sakuntala stood looking at him with growing
despair in her heart ; then, realising from the
King's stony countenance the hopelessness of her
appeal, she fled from the audience-chamber weeping bitterly.

Now although Dushyanta appeared to have
grown wicked and heartless in such a short space
of time, in reality he had only spoken what he
thoroughly believed to be the truth.

SHE FLED FROM THE AUDIENCE CHAMBER
From "Sakuntala, or The Ring of Remembrance"

He did not remember Sakuntala at all, and for this reason—

When the old sage Durvasas had muttered a curse upon the poor girl, he had maliciously decreed, first of all, that she should lose the King's gift, and secondly, that until Dushyanta should see his ring again, he should be unable to remember Sakuntala, even though she stood before him.

Unfortunately not even the god Indra could alter a curse when it had once been pronounced by the old sage, and since Dushyanta's ring had been swept away by the stream in the forest, what hope was there that the King should ever remember his bride?

Nevertheless, in spite of the curse, when Dushyanta thought about the matter in the days that followed, he wished he had treated the poor girl more gently, for he felt that there was some strange mystery concerning her; but it was not until a miracle happened, that he was able to grasp the truth.

Some years after Sakuntala had come to the palace, a fisherman was brought before the King to relate a curious story.

It appeared that the man had caught a fine carp in the river, and when he had opened the

"THE MAN HAD CAUGHT A FINE CARP IN THE RIVER"

fish, lo and behold! a gold ring engraven with the name " Dushyanta " lay within the body of the carp.

The King looked at the ring with a puzzled frown upon his brow.

" It is certainly mine," he said ; " yet I have no recollection of losing it."

He ordered the honest fisherman to be well rewarded, and after examining the ring again he placed it upon his own finger.

" What is this ? " he cried suddenly.   " A cloud seems to be lifted from my mind.   Now I remember—this is the ring I gave to my bride, Sakuntala the hermit maid.   Alas ! what have I done ?   It was Sakuntala who sought me here, and I sent her from me with cruel words."

Memory was fully awakened now, and the King realised with bitterness what grief he had unwittingly brought upon poor innocent Sakuntala.

He hastened to the forest, but the hermitage was deserted, for Father Kanva was no more ; he had the kingdom searched, but it seemed as if Sakuntala had vanished from the earth, and at last the King was forced to believe that the poor girl had died of grief in some unknown spot.

He fell into a deep melancholy from which no one could rouse him, and day and night he sorrowed for his lost bride, while his subjects grieved also at the misery of their beloved King.

But although the god Indra had been powerless to avert the curse of Durvasas, he had not been regardless of the suffering which the angry old sage had caused, and now that Durvasas was unable to work more evil since the ring had been recovered, Indra determined to console the unhappy King.

One day Dushyanta was walking in his garden, thinking of the happy time he had spent in the forest with Sakuntala—so long ago, alas !—when he saw a strange object in the sky which looked like a great shining bird.

Nearer and nearer it came, and to Dushyanta's amazement, the bird proved to be a chariot drawn by prancing horses, whose reins were held by a celestial-looking being.

The car alighted on the earth quite near the King, and the driver called—

" Hail, Dushyanta ! Dost thou not know me ? I am Matali, the charioteer of great Indra. Come with me, for the God hath need of thee."

The King was awestruck, for although Indra had occasionally been known to reveal himself to his worshippers, this was the first time that Dushyanta had been summoned before the holy presence.

He stepped into the chariot and was whirled upwards so swiftly that soon his kingdom lay like a tiny speck beneath him. The car soared still higher, and the horses trod the air as if it were solid ground beneath their feet, until suddenly the chariot stopped in the midst of the clouds, and Matali told Dushyanta to descend.

The King obeyed, and gradually, as the clouds melted away, he saw that he was alone in a peaceful region which was bathed in heavenly light. Birds were singing joyously in the flower-laden trees, and Dushyanta felt that there was something sacred in the air, that surely he was near great Indra's dwelling.

There was a rustling of the bushes, and Dushyanta waited breathlessly. Was the God about to reveal himself?

It was not a heavenly being who appeared, however, but a little boy who was carrying a lion cub, and although the animal struggled fiercely, the child held it closely in his arms without a sign of fear.

"Come hither, boy," cried the King, who was astonished at the bravery of one so young. "Tell me your name."

"I know it not," answered the boy carelessly. "Sometimes they call me 'All-Tamer' because I

have great power over animals,
but it is not my
real name."

"Strange,"
said the King;
"were you my
son you should
bear the princely name of Bharata;" and he
sighed deeply to
think that, had
cruel fate not
separated him
from Sakuntala,
they might have
rejoiced in such
a beautiful,
brave son as
this.   He felt irresistibly drawn towards the boy,
and held out his arms to embrace him, but the
child shrank back crying—

"No one shall touch me.   Mother, mother,
come quickly."

"I am coming, my son," said a gentle voice.
The King started, then began to tremble

violently, for a wild hope had entered his heart—a hope that, almost before he realised it, was fulfilled, for Sakuntala stood before him, Sakuntala, pale and sad-looking, yet even more beautiful than on the day when Dushyanta had first seen her in the forest.

At the sight of the King she drew herself up proudly, but Dushyanta fell at her feet, crying : " O Sakuntala, do not turn from me. Listen, I beseech you ; " and he hurriedly related his strange story, how he had forgotten his bride until the recovery of the ring, and how since that time he had sought her everywhere to make amends for his seemingly wicked conduct.

Sakuntala listened in silence, then her face suddenly lighted up with joy and she cried, " O Dushyanta, now I understand. It must have been the punishment of Durvasas ; " and she told the King what had befallen concerning the angry sage, how she had lost her ring in the stream, and how bitterly she had suffered all these years at the thought of her husband's cruelty towards her.

" But where have you been hidden from me all this time ? What is this place ? " asked Dushyanta eagerly.

" Dear husband, this is a sacred mountain near the dwelling-place of great Indra," Sakuntala

10

answered. " When you denied me in your palace I felt that I should die of grief, but a wonderful thing happened to me. As I lay weeping on the ground, Indra sent his chariot to earth, and I was borne hither by heavenly beings who have watched over me since that time."

" Mother," cried the boy, who had been watching them from a distance, " who is this man ? "

" Your father, my child," replied Sakuntala, with tears of joy in her eyes. " Embrace your son, Dushyanta. He was a gift from the gods to comfort me in my loneliness."

Then, just as the King felt as if his happiness were almost too great to be borne, Matali again appeared in his chariot.

" Art thou satisfied, Dushyanta ? " he cried. " Now, return with me to earth, for it is great Indra's wish. Cherish thy son, oh happy pair, for he shall become the founder of a race of heroes."

The chariot bore them back to earth, and from that time Dushyanta and Sakuntala dwelt in perfect happiness, while their son, whom they named Bharata, grew up to found a noble race, as Matali had foretold.

THE VENGEANCE OF MANASA

ONCE upon a time Manasa and Neta, the daughters of the great God Shiva, came to dwell upon earth for a while, as they had been driven from their celestial home by the jealousy of their stepmother. Neta settled down quite happily as a mortal in a pleasant house by the banks of a river, but Manasa roamed hither and thither in a state of discontent. She wanted power, and although she ruled over all serpents and creeping things she was not satisfied. She desired the worship of mankind, and she devised a plan at last whereby she might secure her object.

In the city of Champaka there lived a wealthy and powerful merchant called Chand who was known to influence the opinions of all his neighbours, and Manasa thought that if she could induce him to pay homage to her, others would soon follow his example.

Now, Chand was the happiest of mortals. He had a gentle, loving wife, six sturdy little sons; he lived in a marble house fit to be the palace of an emperor and his garden was the envy of all who beheld it. Nowhere else in the world, it was

147

said, grew such perfect blossoms and such luscious fruits, and it was Chand's delight, after the heat of the day, to wander amongst his brightly-coloured flowers and laden fruit-trees.

One evening he was sitting alone by his lotus lake when a stranger appeared before him. She was a lovely maiden, youthful and slender, with long, black, snake-like tresses and cold glittering eyes.

Chand arose, saluting her politely, and asked whence she had come and what was her bidding.

" Know, O Chand ! that I am Manasa, daughter of the great Shiva," she answered, " and since I am desirous that men should worship me, I pray you build me a temple in your beautiful garden."

Chand was in no mind to pay homage to Manasa, so he answered that her request was impossible to grant. Already there was a temple to Shiva in his garden, and he did not wish to build another one.

Using all her powers of fascination, the Goddess pleaded with him, but Chand was an obstinate man. When once he had made a decision no one could induce him to alter it, so he repeated firmly that though it grieved him to refuse her request, yet it must be so for many reasons.

At last Manasa grew angry. " You will repent of your folly," she hissed, and away she glided with the stealthy grace of a serpent.

Chand thought no more of the matter and slept peacefully that night, but when he awakened at dawn and leaned out of his window to behold his garden bathed in sunlight, what a sight met his gaze! His beautiful paradise lay in ruins, for in the night strange creeping things had invaded it. Not a leaf was left upon the trees, the blossoms were withered, and no fruit was to be seen upon bough or bush.

" This is the work of Manasa," cried the angry merchant, " but do what she will she shall not triumph over me. Shankara will aid me to outwit her evil schemes."

Shankara was a wise old man who possessed magic powers. At Chand's request he visited the garden, sprinkled the bare trees and withered plants with dew, and, strange to say, in an instant everything was as it had been. The trees burst into leaf, mangoes, pomegranates, and other fruits clustered upon the boughs, and fragrant blossoms unfolded. The birds sang, bees flitted from flower to flower, and Chand rejoiced in his garden once more in the cool of the evening.

The next day, however, he was the most wretched of men, for not only was his garden lying again in ruins, but messengers came beseeching him to follow them to the dwelling of Shankara,

where the good old man lay lifeless with the mark
of a serpent's fang upon his throat.

Chand's sorrow at the loss of his friend was pro-
found. Also there was none now who had power
to revive the ruined garden ; but grief only
heightened the merchant's obstinacy. He vowed
that whatever evil might befall him through the
spite of Manasa, never, never would he propitiate
her. Even when, one by one, his six little sons
died of mysterious ailments, Chand would not give
in. He neglected his business affairs and sat at
home in a darkened room, refusing to be comforted ; and although his heart-broken wife begged
him to reconsider his decision, lest he too should
be struck down, Chand remained obdurate. Then
his wife, fearing for his reason, begged him to set
out upon a trading voyage in order to distract his
mind from sorrow. After much persuasion Chand
agreed to venture forth, but ill-luck pursued him
still. His ships were sunk in a storm, he narrowly
escaped from drowning, and he returned to
Champaka well-nigh a ruined man. But joy
awaited him at home. During his absence his
wife had given birth to a seventh son, and in his
delight at the sight of the child Chand almost
forgot his misery. He set to work to build his
fortunes for the sake of Lakshmindara, as the boy

was called, and his affairs immediately began to prosper.

Now, it really seemed as if the vengeance of Manasa had been completed, for years passed by with only good fortune happening to Chand and his family. Lakshmindara grew into a healthy, handsome youth, and when the time came for him to take a wife, he pleased his parents mightily by his choice of Behulah, the daughter of a neighbouring merchant. Behulah was beloved throughout Champaka for her wisdom, piety, and kindliness, and there was not a soul who did not rejoice at her betrothal to Lakshmindara.

The preparations for the marriage were begun when one night Chand had a terrible dream. Manasa appeared to him and said : " Your son shall die of snake-bite on the night of his marriage."

Chand awakened trembling with fear and told his wife of his disquieting vision. She refused to be alarmed, but Chand was uneasy, for he felt sure that he had had no ordinary dream. Therefore he ordered a steel house to be built for the bridal couple and besought the builders not to leave a crack or hole in any of the walls.

Unfortunately, one of the craftsmen engaged upon the building was a careless man, and when the house was finished he noticed a tiny aperture at the joining of two walls. There was no time to remedy the fault, so he filled in the crack with dust and trusted that no one would notice it.

The wedding ceremony was performed, and, after a magnificent feast, Lakshmindara bore his bride to the steel house. No sooner had he crossed the threshold when a lithe serpent forced its way through the hidden crack in the wall. Behulah gave a cry of alarm, and Lakshmindara, saying : " There is nothing to fear, beloved," advanced to kill the intruder. But before he could draw his sword the serpent had attacked him and buried its poisoned fang in his throat.

Lakshmindara fell to the ground lifeless and the serpent disappeared through the crack in the wall.

Behulah's screams were heard by the guards outside the steel house. They rushed in, but there was nothing to be done. Chand was summoned, and, broken-hearted at this dreadful blow, he ordered the funeral pyre to be prepared.

But Behulah clung to him and, amidst her sobs, begged him not to consign her husband's body to the flames.

" Alas, my child ! " answered Chand brokenly, " what can we do now but give him honourable burial ? "

" I have heard that those who die of snake-bite

may yet be brought back to life," cried Behulah. " It may be that we can find some magician who will perform the miracle. Place the body upon a raft, I beseech you, and let me sail away alone with my sad burden in search of help."

Chand protested that such a miracle was impossible, but Behulah answered: " Nothing is impossible for the Gods to perform."

So Chand could not but accede to her request.

The body of Lakshmindara was placed upon a raft and Behulah seated herself beside the dead man ; then the raft was loosened from its moorings and it drifted down the river while Behulah prayed ceaselessly to the Gods to restore her husband to life.

But no magician appeared to help her. Still she did not lose faith, and when, after some days, the raft ran aground near a pleasant dwelling-place, Behulah said to herself: " Here perhaps shall I find one who will aid me."

There was no one in the house, however, except a beautiful woman, who greeted Behulah kindly and listened to her sad story.

Now, this strange woman happened to be Neta, the sister of Manasa, and knowing this wantonly cruel death to be the work of the Snake Goddess, Neta was full of anger against her sister.

"Alas, poor Behulah!" she said gently, "I have no power to restore the dead to life, but I will call upon my father, great Shiva, who will surely aid you."

So Neta invoked the presence of the Great One, and there, in the midst of a blinding light, stood the God. Behulah pleaded with him and Shiva was moved at the sound of her sweet voice; then she danced before him with such grace that Shiva cried: "You deserve nothing but joy, O beautiful Behulah! Therefore will I restore your husband to life."

So Shiva breathed upon the body and Lakshmindara opened his eyes and gave a cry of joy at the sight of Behulah. Then great Shiva said: "Return to Champaka and fear no more the vengeance of Manasa. It shall be averted, by my decree, from the house of Chand and his descendants for evermore."

The united lovers set out upon their homeward way and the rejoicings at their return were a thousand times greater than those on their wedding day. Thenceforward Lakshmindara and Behulah lived in joy and peace, and Chand was once more a happy man. He prospered in all his undertakings, and the new garden which he designed for himself was even more beautiful than the old one had been.

THE ADVENTURES OF RAMA AND SITA

PART I

THE BANISHMENT OF RAMA

ALL through the long summer night, the people of Ayodhya laboured to deck their fair city for the morrow's festival, the coronation of their beloved Prince Rama. They hung gay lanterns from the treetops and adorned the white temples of the city with banners and glittering streamers; they burned fragrant incense and strewed flowers upon all sides, and, amongst all the merry crowds in the streets, there was not a soul who did not look forward to the coming festival with joy, for Rama and his young wife Sita were the idols of the people's hearts.

Now, although Rama was to be crowned, his father, King Dasaratha, was still alive, but the old monarch now felt too enfeebled to perform his royal duties unaided, so, from his three sons Rama, Bharat, and Lakshman, he had chosen Rama his firstborn to share the throne with him henceforward.

Unfortunately for Rama, however, he had two dangerous enemies in the royal palace, through no fault of his own. They were Queen Kaikeyi, his stepmother, and her old slave called Manthara, who was devoted to her mistress and knew all her secrets, and on this night of joyous preparation, the two women were standing at a window in the palace, looking gloomily at the crowded streets below them.

"Ah, Manthara," Queen Kaikeyi cried bitterly.

" would that these preparations were for mine own son, Bharat, instead of for Rama, the King's favourite."

" Methinks thy wish can yet be granted, lady," said Manthara, with a cunning smile. " Is not Prince Bharat also beloved by his father, the King ? "

" How, woman ? " asked the Queen impatiently. " Dost thou think, then, that Dasaratha would place Bharat before Rama at *my* bidding ? "

" Stranger things even than this have come to pass," said Manthara ; and she reminded Kaikeyi how, years ago, the Queen had saved King Dasaratha's life by tending his wounds upon a battlefield, and how, in return, the grateful monarch had sworn to grant her two favours at any time that she should ask for them.

" Never yet hast thou claimed thy rights," continued Manthara, " but the time hath come for thy requests to be made. Listen, my Queen."

Then, drawing nearer to her mistress, she whispered a few words in her ear which made the Queen's eyes glitter with triumph.

" O wise Manthara ! " she cried, " I will do as thou hast advised ; " and, as the dawn was now at hand and there was no time to be lost since the festival would begin soon after sunrise, Kaikeyi hastened to the King's apartment.

" My lord," she cried eagerly to the old monarch, who was reclining upon his couch, " tell me this ! Dost thou remember how I saved thy life upon the battlefield long ago ? "

" Never have I forgotten thy loving skill," answered the King, " nor that I did make thee a promise at that time. Hast thou come to demand thy two favours now, my Kaikeyi ? "

The Queen bowed her head in eager assent.

" Ask thy boons of me now," said the unsuspecting Dasaratha, " and I swear by my dear son Rama, that if it be within my power to grant thy requests, thou shalt be denied nothing."

" Then," cried Kaikeyi in triumph, " grant me these two things, O King. Let our son Bharat be crowned this day, and let Rama be banished to the forest of Dandak for fourteen years."

Dasaratha nearly swooned with dismay and anger.

" What sayest thou ? " he cried in trembling tones. " Thou traitress ! What wrong hath my Rama ever done to thee ? Nay, these infamous requests shall not be granted."

" As thou wilt," replied Kaikeyi with assumed carelessness, " but think not, Dasaratha, that thy

subjects shall remain in ignorance of thy broken pledge to me. Thou shalt ever be known throughout these vast lands as a King who hath failed to keep his solemn vow, and nations hereafter shall hold thee in scorn."

Dasaratha knew that he was in the Queen's power, for under all circumstances must a King be true to his word, and besides, had he not vowed, in the name of his dear son, that he would grant the requests, cruel and wicked though they had proved to be ? Vainly he begged the Queen to ask him any other favour excepting the banishment of Rama, but the Queen was obdurate. She thought that if Rama were sent to Dandak, which was a forest said to be thronged by evil spirits, it was very unlikely that he would return from there alive after fourteen years' banishment, and thus Bharat would be able to reign unmolested over vast Kosala, the country of which Ayodhya was the capital.

At last, finding his entreaties were powerless to alter the Queen's decree, Dasaratha resigned himself to his fate, and, with an aching heart, he entered the great audience-chamber in the palace where eager crowds were awaiting him.

To the amazement of every one in the hall (excepting Kaikeyi and Manthara, of course) the King announced that henceforth Bharat, not Rama, was to share his throne. There were murmurs of surprise and dismay from the people, and Prince Rama, with wonder in his eyes, stepped forward ; then the excited crowds began to cheer him as he stood before the throne—a noble, handsome figure, with truth and courage stamped upon his brow.

" What have I done, my father ? " he asked with simple dignity, " that thou shouldst thus dishonour me ? "

The King could no longer control his grief. Amidst bitter tears he spoke of his vow to Kaikeyi —how her demands must be granted, cruel and unjust though they might be.

" Worse tidings have I yet to relate, my son," he continued in despairing tones. " Not only must I deprive thee of the throne, but it is the desire of thy stepmother that thou shalt be banished to the forest of Dandak for fourteen years."

" Shame upon the false Queen ! " cried the people with one voice, and Bharat, seizing Rama's hand, vowed that he would never supplant his stepbrother upon the throne.

But Rama, who had listened to his father's words in silence, now said sorrowfully—

" Nay, good Bharat, the crown is thine, for I must abide by our father's promise. Alone will I seek the forest of Dandak, and not until fourteen years have passed over our heads, will I return to Ayodhya."

" Thou shalt not go alone, my Rama," cried a sweet voice, and beautiful dark-eyed Sita, who until this moment had been overcome by grief and fear at the strange tidings of King Dasaratha, now rushed to her husband's side and flung her arms around his neck.

" Let me share thine exile," she continued imploringly, " for I should surely die here without thee."

" But the woods of Dandak are full of peril,"

II

answered Rama gently. " Thou knowest well, my Sita, that dread Ravana, the King of the Demons, is said to haunt the forest with his wicked hosts, who are ever desirous of working evil upon the good and innocent."

" Then I will also accompany thee, Rama," cried Prince Lakshman, the King's youngest son, who had always been devoted to Rama. " I will help thee to protect thy Sita with all my power."

First of all Rama protested that he could not allow his wife and brother to endure the hardships of a forest life, but Sita and Lakshman were so earnest in their entreaties to accompany him, that at last he gave way to them. Then he turned to the King, and embracing the old man tenderly, he cried—

" Fare thee well, my father. I blame thee not, for thou hast been the victim of my stepmother's cunning."

So, amidst great sorrowing, Rama, Sita and Lakshman took leave of all those who loved them in the palace, and, after changing their royal robes for the plain attire of forest folk, they set out towards the deep, dark woods of Dandak which lay south of the kingdom of Kosala.

Scarcely had the three exiles left the palace, when King Dasaratha fell into a swoon from which all his physicians failed to revive him, and after several days he passed away without regaining consciousness.

" Now," thought false Kaikeyi, " my Bharat will be crowned at last."

But the Queen was doomed to bitter disappointment, for Bharat refused to ascend the throne, saying that Rama must be brought back from the forest to take his rightful place as the King. Kaikeyi implored her son not to frustrate her plans for his glory, but Bharat was determined to see justice done, so he journeyed in haste to the forest of Dandak, where he managed to overtake Rama and his companions.

So far the hardships of life in the forest did not seem to have troubled the exiles, for Rama and Lakshman were glowing with health and good spirits, while Sita looked more beautiful than ever in her simple garb. Rama was deeply grieved to hear of his father's death, and he refused to listen to Bharat's entreaty that he should now return to Ayodhya to be crowned King of Kosala.

" My father pledged his word that I should remain in banishment for fourteen years," he said firmly ; " therefore I will remain here in fulfilment of his vow."

" Then will I govern the people as thy regent,"

cried Bharat, " until the joyful day when thou wilt return."

So Bharat took leave of the wanderers and, returning to Ayodhya, he governed the vast country of Kosala with wisdom and justice ; but, true to his word, he refused to be crowned, and he set a pair of Rama's shoes upon the throne as a sign of his absent brother's authority.

Thus Kaikeyi had failed to make her son a real King, but neither she nor Manthara gave up hope, for they felt sure that Rama would never return from the grim forest of Dandak.

Meanwhile the exiles penetrated deeper in the woods, living upon herbs, fruits and venison. Sometimes they came across a tiny hermitage wherein dwelt some holy man who gave them hospitality, otherwise they saw not a living soul in the forest, and although they were ever on their guard against the demon King Ravana and his hosts, so far not a single evil spirit had appeared to molest them.

Thus time passed by with surprising rapidity until the wanderers had spent nearly ten years of their exile in the forest, and one day they chanced to arrive at a little hermitage which was inhabited by an old priest of great repute, named Agastya.

The holy man welcomed them cordially, and

was astonished to hear that they had spent so many years in the forest without having been attacked by the demons.

"Since I am a priest, Ravana and his wicked hosts molest me not," he said; "but many a time have I seen them lurking near this spot, and I fear lest ye may be persecuted by them. Perchance, Rama, thou hast been  destined by the Gods to wage war upon these evil spirits who trouble the earth so sorely. I will give thee my store of weapons."

Then, to Rama's delight, Agastya presented him with a bow and a quiver full of an endless store of arrows, while Lakshman's heart was gladdened by the gift of a golden-sheathed sword.

" These weapons at one time belonged to the great God Indra," explained Agastya, " and their aim is true and deadly. Now ye may wander where ye will, for the demons are fearful of these arrows and this sword."

Rama and Lakshman did not know how to thank the old priest sufficiently, and as Rama touched his new treasures with loving fingers, he solemnly vowed to himself that if ever the opportunity should come to him, he would try to rid the world of these evil spirits.

The exiles rested for a while at the hermitage, then they took leave of Agastya, and Rama asked the old priest if he would direct them to some pleasant spot, where they might settle down for the coming winter.

" Sita hath grown weary of our wanderings," he said, " therefore we would build ourselves a little dwelling-place."

" Seek the Vale of Panchavati," answered Agastya. " It is a pleasant, fruitful glade wherein ye may all dwell in comfort and peace."

Then the old man told them in which direction they would find the vale, and the wanderers took leave of him and continued on their journey, armed with the precious weapons.

Soon they reached the Vale of Panchavati,

which was indeed a beautiful, tranquil spot. It was covered with blossoming shrubs and trees in whose branches the birds sang unceasingly, and a little stream wound its way through the glade with a pleasant rippling sound.

" Let us remain here," cried Sita eagerly, so the Princes laboured to build her a little dwelling, and before very long their task was accomplished. Sita was as delighted with her new home as if it had been a palace, although the walls of the hut were made of hardened earth instead of marble, and, in the place of gleaming columns, pillars of bamboo upheld the thatched roof.

Winter slipped away peacefully, and Rama now felt convinced that the demons would never trouble them, since Agastya had armed them with his magic weapons ; but he was soon to find out his mistake, and to learn by bitter experience that magic weapons alone were insufficient to protect the good and innocent from the spells of King Ravana.

PART II

THE CAPTURE OF SITA

ALAS for Rama and his companions ! With the return of Spring came the end of their happiness

and peace, for dread Ravana, the King of the demons, was now determined to wreak evil upon them, since he was the sworn foe of Gods and virtuous mortals. Ravana knew that the sage Agastya had given Rama and Laksh-man the magic weapons, therefore the demon King realised that it would be dangerous for him to attack the brothers openly, and that he must find some means of slaying them by stealth. So he constantly lurked unseen near the Vale of Panchavati, in the hope of meeting the brothers unarmed, but never yet had he caught sight of them without their precious weapons.

However, one evening in the early Spring, while Ravana was watching the exiles from a distance, an idea came to him which filled his evil heart with joy.

" This Sita is fair above all women," he cried to himself, " and she is dearer to Rama than his very life. No longer will I seek to slay this proud Prince, but I will steal from him his most cherished possession. Sita shall be mine ! "

The longer Ravana pondered over this wicked scheme, the more it delighted him, although he knew that the capture of Sita would be no easy task, for neither Rama nor Lakshman ever left her unguarded for one moment. Still, Ravana had all the aids of sorcery at his command, and he determined to ask the help of his brother Marichi, who was the wisest and most cunning of all the demon race.

Marichi dwelt alone in a distant part of the forest, so Ravana summoned his chariot to convey him thither without delay. At the demon King's word of command, the chariot appeared instantly. It was a golden vehicle drawn by two fierce-looking asses with goblins' heads, and, not only could this strange car roll over the ground with incredible swiftness, but it was also able to fly through the air like a great bird. Ravana stepped inside his car, and, while Rama and his companions were resting contentedly after the day's labours, little dreaming of the sorrow in store for them, the demon King flew in his chariot to the most gloomy part of the forest, where Marichi sat before his dwelling, studying his magic art.

"Hail, Marichi!" cried Ravana. "I have come to seek thine aid. Knowest thou that Rama, Prince of Kosala, hath dared to enter this forest with Sita, his wife, and his brother Lakshman?"

"Ay, Ravana," answered Marichi gloomily, "but take heed! Do not molest these mortals, for I have a strange feeling in my heart that this Rama will bring evil upon us."

Ravana laughed contemptuously at his brother's words, but Marichi continued in solemn tones—

"Methinks that the Gods themselves have sent this powerful Prince to destroy us. Dost thou know, Ravana, that the magic arrows of Agastya are in his possession?"

"Well do I know this thing," answered Ravana. "Therefore have I no mind to fight with this Rama. But listen, my Marichi! What I am about to accomplish will injure him more than death."

Then, with malicious glee, Ravana told his brother how he intended to carry Sita away to his enchanted palace upon the distant island of Lanka.

"There shall she become my Queen," he cried.

"And Rama shall seek for her in vain, for no mortal can cross the turbulent seas which divide Lanka from this land."

"Thou shalt have no aid from me, brother," said Marichi firmly, "for I know that disaster will befall us, shouldst thou attempt to injure Rama. Let this Sita be, I implore thee; thou canst find another bride even more beautiful, perchance, than the wife of Rama."

Ravana was not to be thwarted by his brother, however, and as he knew that he would never be able to carry out his scheme without the aid of Marichi, the demon King tried to gain his end by bribery.

"I will give thee half my kingdom if thou wilt help me," he cried; but Marichi was not to be tempted by this offer, so at last Ravana grew

desperate, and, raising his sword, he shouted, "Refuse thine aid and thou shalt die instantly."

Seeing that Ravana was in deadly earnest, Marichi was forced to give in, and the two demons now plotted together for such a long while that it was not until daybreak that they set out in Ravana's chariot, with all their infamous plans in readiness.

Meanwhile, the dreams of Rama and his companions had been quite unshadowed by presages of evil, and they were now enjoying the beauties of the Spring morning. They busied themselves light-heartedly with their tasks, and at noon, Lakshman wandered a little way from the glade in search of fresh fruits, while Rama and Sita sat down to rest beneath a shady tree.

Sita gazed admiringly at the Spring blossoms all around her, and Rama watched her sweet face with loving eyes, thinking of the devotion and courage which had caused her to share his exile. He was wondering how he would ever be able to repay her for her unselfish love, when she gave a sudden start.

"Look, my Rama," she cried, pointing to a young gazelle which had just bounded into sight. "See the beautiful little creature! What a graceful form it hath, and what a shining coat. Never did I see so lovely an animal. How lightly it skips from place to place amongst

the gorge-ous blos-soms, how happy in the golden sunshine in this peace-ful place! Oh grace-ful, beautiful little creature, with shining coat—like living gold! Would that it were mine!"

"What wouldst thou do with the little animal then?" asked Rama.

"I would make it my playfellow," she answered wistfully, "and when the long years of our exile have passed by, the little creature should return with me to Ayodhya."

"Thou shalt have thy desire," cried Rama, and he darted in pursuit of the gazelle, but the timid little animal sprang back and hid itself among the trees.

Sita gave a little cry of disappointment, and the gazelle reappeared, only to elude Rama's grasp once more by springing still further into the thicket.

"I will catch the animal for thee, never fear," said Rama reassuringly. "Ho, Lakshman! Come hither and guard Sita while I pursue this gazelle."

At his brother's call Lakshman hurried back to the glade, and Rama, seizing his bow and arrows, sped swiftly after the gazelle, which was darting hither and thither in a most tantalising fashion. First of all it led Rama through the thicket, then it rushed onward far into the forest, so far, indeed, that the Prince began to grow hot and weary, but he would not give up the pursuit.

" This is the first thing Sita hath desired since we have dwelt in the forest," he told himself, " and, if it be within my power to grant it, she shall have her wish."

On bounded the gazelle, now venturing near Rama, now hiding itself from view, until at last, when he realised how far he had travelled from the Vale of Panchavati, Rama began to feel uneasy.

" These are not the wiles of an innocent crea-ture," he thought. " What if it be some trick of the demons to lure me from the side of Sita ! The Gods be praised that Lakshman is with her." Once more the gazelle darted to-wards him, then, as Rama raised his hand, it sprang back like a flash of light-ning.

" Nay," said the perplexed Prince, " even though I were

to capture this animal, it would be no fit play-mate for my Sita, therefore I will slay the creature and return to her with the bright fur instead of the living gazelle."

So Rama drew his bow and let fly one of his magic arrows. Immediately the animal fell to the ground, and as Rama drew near with a pang of remorse for having injured such a beautiful little creature, a strange thing happened !

The gazelle began to change its shape, and rapidly assumed the form of a demon with a deadly wound in his side !

It was Marichi who, by means of his sorcery, had turned himself into a gazelle, hoping to lure both Rama and Lakshman from the side of Sita.

Half of the demon's work had already been accomplished, for here was Rama, far away from his beloved wife ; but, as he looked upon the Prince with eyes of hatred, Marichi made one supreme effort to finish the task that Ravana had set him.

" Help, Lakshman, help ! " he shouted in a voice which was exactly like the voice of Rama ; then the demon fell back lifeless, whilst Rama stood by with wonder and disquiet in his heart.

Now Marichi's dying cry had echoed through the forest (just as the demon had intended), far away to the Vale of Pan-chavati, where Sita and Laksh-man were awaiting the return of Rama, and, at the gruesome sound, Sita looked at her companion in terror.

"'Twas the voice of Rama!" she cried. "He is in peril! Go quicklyto him Lakshman."

But Lakshman shook his head.

"Nay, Sita," he answered gravely. "I cannot leave thee, for I have pledged my word to Rama that I will ever remain with thee when he is absent."

"Go, go, I implore thee," Sita cried in tears.

12

"Of what value can be my life if my lord be slain? Hasten, brother, lest thou shouldst be too late."

"Calm thy fears," he said gently.   "'Twas but the voice of some evil spirit in the forest.   Why should Rama, the fearless and the invincible, call for my help?   He can ever protect himself with the magic arrows of Agastya."

But Sita wrung her hands in anguish and refused to be comforted.

"Art thou then a coward?" she cried bitterly. "Oh, I see it now—thou *fearest* to aid thy brother."

Lakshman could not endure this unjust taunt.

"So be it, my sister," he said sorrowfully.   "I will go."

Then, imploring her not to leave the hut whatever might happen, he hurried away in the direction whence the mysterious cry had seemed to come.

Sita watched his departure with mingled relief and terror.   She was not afraid to be left alone, but she dreaded lest Lakshman should arrive too late upon the scene to help Rama, and she bitterly upbraided herself for her foolish whim which had been the cause of peril—perhaps even death—to her beloved Rama.

The moments passed by, and each one seemed like an hour to poor Sita as she crouched by the hut, watching every movement of the trees, and listening intently for the sound of footsteps. Presently she heard a rustling amongst the bushes, and she sprang to her feet, but, alas! for her eager hopes—a man appeared in sight, but he was neither Rama nor Lakshman, only an old hermit with bowed shoulders and weary tread.

The old man drew near, and Sita noticed, with a pang of fear, that a change had suddenly stolen over the forest. Until that moment the sun had shone and the birds had cheered her with their merry songs; now there was nothing to be heard from the trees, not a leaf rustled in the bushes, and overhead the sky was grey and gloomy.

" Hail, lady," said the stranger in feeble tones. " May I rest awhile in this pleasant spot? for I am weary and footsore."

Trying to stifle her fears, Sita greeted the old man courteously, but oh, how she longed for the return of Rama and Lakshman, because there was something about the stranger's bearing which chilled her very soul!

" I will bring thee water for thy feet and fruits for thy refreshment," she said timidly, and the old man thanked her, gazing steadfastly at her the while, with eyes that were curiously bright and piercing for his age.

" Who art thou, lady?" he asked. " And why

dost thou dwell in this dangerous, lonesome forest ? Thy beauty and grace should adorn a palace, not this rude hut.''

Sita, shrinking still more from the flattery in his words, told him hurriedly how she had chosen to share the exile of her husband, and when she explained that her fancy for the gazelle had caused both Rama and Lakshman to leave her side, the old man smiled with joy. Then he stood upright, and a change took place in him—his shrunken height increased to a mighty stature, his aged countenance grew youthful, bold and evil-looking, and his hermit's garb fell to the ground, revealing the regal attire beneath, for it was none other than the King of the demons who stood there—dread Ravana himself !

At these strange happenings Sita drew back with a cry of terror, but Ravana said reassuringly : '' Have no fear, Sita, I will not harm thee. Know that I am Ravana, King of the enchanted Isle of Lanka, and I have come hither to make thee my Queen. Thou shalt dwell in my beautiful palace, and thy days shall be full of delight. Come with me, thou fairest of women.''

He stretched out his arms, but Sita shrank from him, crying proudly : '' Dost thou not know that I am the wife of peerless Rama ? ''

"Rama will never return to thee," answered Ravana, "for doubtless my brother Marichi hath slain him. 'Twas Marichi himself who did take the form of a gazelle in order to lure thy Rama deep into the forest."

Sita did not know whether to believe these cruel words or not; she gazed piteously at Ravana, trying to read his countenance, but she saw nothing but malicious joy and triumph written upon it.

"If my lord be slain, then," she said bravely, "I will ever be true to his memory. Go, thou wicked King, and leave me to mourn in peace."

"I go not without thee," Ravana answered, and he gave a low cry, whereupon his magic chariot appeared; then, heedless of Sita's tears and entreaties, he seized her in his mighty arms and forced her to enter the chariot.

Immediately the car began to soar upwards, and poor Sita felt that all was lost.

"Thou canst carry me away," she cried desperately, "but never will I become thy Queen. I will be faithful to Rama whether he be living or dead."

Ravana's only reply was to urge his steeds to travel faster, for he saw in the distance a dark speck flying towards the car, and he feared that already some one was pursuing him.

Nearer came this strange object, and Ravana recognised that it was Jatayu, the King of the Vultures, who had always been an enemy of the demon race.

"Stay, Ravana," cried the great bird as he soared above the chariot. "Whither bearest thou this unwilling captive?"

"O good Vulture, help me!" pleaded Sita breathlessly. "I am Sita, the wife of Rama, and this cruel King hath captured me by cunning and force."

"Release her," commanded the vulture; but the demon King answered scornfully—

"Never at *thy* bidding! Out of my way, thou insolent Jatayu, else I will surely slay thee."

Jatayu hurled himself fiercely upon Ravana, but, alas! the demon King's spear was thrust deeply into his side.

"O Sita, I cannot help thee now," moaned the poor vulture. "May the Gods protect thee"; and gasping with pain and despair, Jatayu sank down to the earth far below, while Ravana laughed with triumph, and again urged his steeds to travel swiftly.

The chariot floated on, beyond the forest, above plains and hills, until it reached a mountain, upon the top of which Sita caught a glimpse of some beings who looked like huge apes. The car paused for one instant in its flight, and Sita, guided by a sudden impulse, loosened her scarf and necklace and let both the ornaments fall into the hands of the creatures beneath her.

"Perchance if Rama be living, he will wander here in search of me," she thought sadly, "and those apes may give him my scarf and necklace and tell him in which direction the chariot did fly."

Onward the car pursued its dizzy flight, over villages and cities, until at last it approached the sea coast; then away it flew far above the turbulent ocean, to the island of Lanka, where poor Sita was destined to spend several years of sorrow and loneliness.

PART III

HANUMAN TO THE RESCUE

AFTER the strange death of the demon Marichi, Rama hastened back to the Vale of Panchavati, but before he had travelled half the distance his heart grew heavy with dread, for he met Lakshman hurrying towards him with a troubled bearing.

"Where is Sita?" Rama shouted eagerly. "Thou hast not left her unguarded?"

Lakshman began to explain what had occurred,

but Rama interrupted him with the reproachful cry—

" O Lakshman, thou hast done ill! Come quickly, there is evil abroad in the forest."

With frantic haste the brothers rushed onward, and when they drew near the vale they called loudly Sita's name, but, alas! there was no reply!

Wild-eyed with terror, Rama stumbled through the glade, only to find, when he reached the hut, that his worst fears were realised, for the little dwelling was chill and empty, and although his cries of "Sita! Sita!" re-echoed through the vale, not a sound came to comfort him.

" The demons have stolen her," groaned poor Rama, rushing to and fro in a frenzied manner. " 'Tis the work of Ravana and his fiendish hosts."

" Nay, Rama, believe not such a terrible thing," faltered Lakshman. " Sita may be sleeping, wearied by thy long absence. Let us seek her by the stream where the blue lotus doth bloom ; 'tis her favourite haunt."

But Sita was not resting by the water, neither was she hidden in any nook or glen in the leafy vale, and though the brothers searched for her unceasingly, they could find not a trace of her mysterious flight. Darkness fell and still they continued their pursuit, growing wan and haggard as the hours slipped by ; and when at length the sun rose upon a new day, Rama gave way to his despair.

" O Lakshman, why didst thou leave her ? " he moaned, flinging himself upon the ground in his anguish. " My gentle, loving Sita ! What hath become of thee ? I shall never see thee again."

" Do not lose hope yet, my brother," said Lakshman ; " even though thy Sita be in the hands of Ravana, we will discover the demon King and wrest her from his wicked grasp. Come, let us continue our search."

" Whither shall we go ? " asked Rama helplessly.

"Towards the south," answered Lakshman, "for I have oft heard it said that the kingdom of Ravana lieth far away in that direction. Come, brother. Perchance we may hear aught of the demons upon our journey."

Rama suffered himself to be led in a southerly direction, and before long the wisdom of Lakshman's suggestion was clearly proved, for, across their path, the brothers discovered a huge vulture, who was bleeding to death from a gaping wound in his side.

It was Jatayu, and as Rama and Lakshman approached, the bird raised his head with an effort and cried feebly: "Are ye searching for Sita, the wife of Rama?"

"Hast thou seen her?" was Rama's breathless answer. "Oh, speak, noble bird—speak quickly!"

"'Twas in her defence that I gained this wound," gasped Jatayu. "Ravana hath taken her in his chariot——"

"Whither? Tell me whither?" pleaded Rama, vainly trying to staunch poor Jatayu's wound.

"Southwards," whispered the bird faintly. "Towards the mountain of Rishyamuka—seek the aid of Sugriva, the Vanar King——"

A quiver ran through Jatayu's mighty frame,

then he lay motionless, and Rama realised with deep sorrow that the noble bird was dead.

In order to show their gratitude and respect for such a good and generous being, Rama and Lakshman gave the body of Jatayu an honourable burial; then, with a faint spark of hope in their hearts, they set out to find the mountain of Rishyamuka. For many days their way still lay through the dark forest, but at last they reached open country once more, and, beyond the wide plain which stretched before them, they could perceive a lofty mountain in the distance.

" See, Rama, there lieth Rishyamuka," cried Lakshman hopefully, and Rama answered—

" The Gods grant that thy words be true, brother. Let us journey thither."

They hastened towards this wooded height, and just as they were about to ascend the mountain-slope in the hope of finding this Sugriva, of whom Jatayu had spoken, a huge ape appeared from a dense thicket to bar their way.

" Not so fast," cried the great animal fiercely. " I am Hanuman, the counsellor of King Sugriva, who dwelleth upon this mount, and, ere ye pass, ye must tell me why ye have come hither."

In spite of his ugly appearance and rough manner, there was something benevolent in

Hanuman's countenance, and Rama, feeling instinctively that he had found a friend, began to relate his story. To his joy he soon learned that, not only had Hanuman seen the chariot of Ravana flying southward, but that a woman in the car had flung down her ornaments, which had actually fallen into the hands of Hanuman himself. The ape proudly produced these treasures, whereupon Rama could hardly restrain his tears, for he recognised the silken scarf and the glittering necklace as Sita's own belongings.

"So ye seek the aid of Sugriva," said Hanuman, when Rama had finished his sorrowful tale. "Come with me to my master, then."

As the kindly ape led Rama and Lakshman up the mountain-slope, he told them that Sugriva was really the King of the great monkey tribes called Vanars, but that his wicked brother Bali had driven him from his kingdom of Kishkinda and had usurped the throne for himself. In despair Sugriva had fled to the mountain of Rishyamuka, where he had dwelt in exile for some years, deserted by all his subjects excepting a few faithful warriors, of whom Hanuman was the chief.

" Perchance ye may help Sugriva to recover his throne," said the ape, " then gladly will my master raise an army to attack Ravana, for the demons have ever been the enemies of our race."

At the top of the mountain sat the exiled King Sugriva, brooding fiercely over his wrongs, and when he had listened to the story of Rama a gleam of hope lightened his mournful countenance.

" If thou dost possess mighty weapons, O Rama," he said, " I beseech thee to help me, for it is beyond my power to subdue the strength and cunning of my brother Bali alone."

Rama gladly promised his assistance, whereupon Sugriva, in return, pledged his word that, should he be established once more upon his throne, he would send armies of Vanars to scour the earth in search of Sita.

Rama begged that no time should be lost, so he and Lakshman, escorted by their Vanar friends, journeyed without delay to the kingdom of Kishkinda. When the usurper Bali heard that his brother Sugriva was advancing against him, he rushed forward to meet him in a furious rage, and the two powerful apes fell upon each other with cries of hatred and revenge. First of all Rama stood by, hoping that Sugriva would be able to overcome Bali unaided, but soon it was evident that the usurper was gaining the victory, and in order to save Sugriva from a deadly blow, Rama let fly one of his magic arrows, which struck Bali dead in an instant.

Then Hanuman called upon the Vanars to rally round their former King, and since they had all grown weary of Bali's rule, the Vanar tribes received Sugriva with joy and enthusiasm.

The King professed his undying gratitude to Rama, and pledged his word that, as soon as he had established peace and order in his kingdom, he would send forth great armies in search of Ravana and Sita ; but, unfortunately, Sugriva was so elated by the joys of his newly-restored monarchy, that he spent his time in feasting and enjoyment, and many months passed without there being any preparations made for the discovery of the demon King.

At last Hanuman, who was ashamed of his master's dishonourable conduct, managed to persuade Sugriva to keep his word, so four mighty armies of Vanars were despatched north, south, east and west of the land of Kishkinda in order to discover, if possible, where Ravana had hidden Sita.

Rama awaited the return of these armies with frenzied eagerness, but, to his dismay, all the forces, excepting the division which had gone southward, returned without any tidings whatsoever of Ravana and his captive.

Rama was now forced to put all his faith in the southern army which was commanded by Hanuman, but so many months passed by without the return of this division, that there was grave fear in the land of Kishkinda lest disaster should have befallen the brave Vanars.

However, although Hanuman and his army had encountered many dangers upon their travels, they were still unharmed ; but as Hanuman had made a vow that he would never return without tidings of Sita, he led his forces further and further south, through swamp and jungle, over hill and plain to within sight of the ocean which washed the shores of the land, and here at last he was rewarded for his tireless search.

Upon the top of a mountain he found an old vulture called Sampati, the brother of that good Jatayu who had lost his life in the defence of Sita. Sampati had singed his wings in a bold attempt to fly over the sun, and he was now resting to recover from his injuries ; but he told Hanuman that ere he had fallen from the dizzy heights to which he had ascended, he had seen the chariot of Ravana alighting upon the shores of the island of Lanka.

" There was a struggling captive in the chariot," continued Sampati, " who must have been this very Sita, whom thou seekest, but I fear that thou wilt never be able to rescue her."

" Wherefore not ? " cried Hanuman, gaily.

" I will lead my brave Vanars to Lanka and the demons shall flee before us."

" But thou and thy Vanars can never reach the island," said Sampati, " for it is encompassed by perilous seas which none save Ravana and his demons have yet been able to ford."

But Hanuman's joy was not to be spoilt by Sampati's words, and, instead of returning to Rama with his good tidings, the brave ape determined to visit Lanka by himself, in order to discover how strong the demons were, and what would be the best way of rescuing Sita. So leaving his army to rest awhile, Hanuman slipped away to the sea coast, where, unfortunately, he found that Sampati's warning was only too true, for although he could descry the island of Lanka, in the distance, the sea which divided it from the mainland was quite impassable. Hanuman was not to be deterred from his object, however, and he soon thought of a likely way out of this difficulty.

He had always been famed for his extraordinary prowess in leaping, and he decided to make one desperate effort to spring over the raging waters, even though the attempt should cost him his life. Therefore, without hesitating, he climbed to the top of a rock, gave one flying

13

leap, and, to his joy and relief, he found himself upon the shore of Lanka.

Dazed by his effort, Hanuman looked about him, and was astonished that such an evil place should be so beautiful. The soft grass at his feet was studded with flowers, the trees around him bore both blossom and fruit at the same time, and in the distance shone the golden walls and white turrets of a city—the home of dread Ravana.

" Doubtless Sita is hidden within yonder city," said Hanuman to himself; " but I will await nightfall ere I begin my search."

So he lingered outside the city until all was dim and quiet within, then, since he was fearful that his huge size might attract attention, he changed himself into a tiny monkey and nimbly scaled the golden walls until he found himself at last within the enchanted city.

The broad streets were guarded by grim-looking sentinels, but they did not perceive the little monkey, who sped swiftly to the portals of a palace wherein he hoped to find Sita.

He hurried through rich ante-rooms where hideous demons lay sleeping until he reached a spacious apartment adorned with gold and precious stones. Here, upon a crystal daïs, reclined dread Ravana, wrapped in deep slumber, and as Hanuman gazed at the unconscious monarch, he longed to put an end to his evil life.

But there was work to be accomplished before he might attack Ravana, so Hanuman crept away noiselessly to the women's apartments, and he looked eagerly at the sleeping faces there; but they were all so ugly and horrible to behold, that he knew that Sita was not amongst them.

He continued his search, but, after investigating the whole of the palace, he was still unsuccessful. So he came out into the moonlight once more, wondering in which one of the many mansions in the city Sita could be concealed.

Suddenly he caught a glimpse of a little white pavilion, half hidden in a grove of asoca trees;

and feeling that this might be a likely place, he hastened thither. When he peeped through the latticed window, he could hardly restrain a cry of triumph, for there, surrounded by a guard of female demons, lay the most beautiful woman he had ever beheld, and he knew that Sita was found at last.

She was not asleep, for he could hear the sound

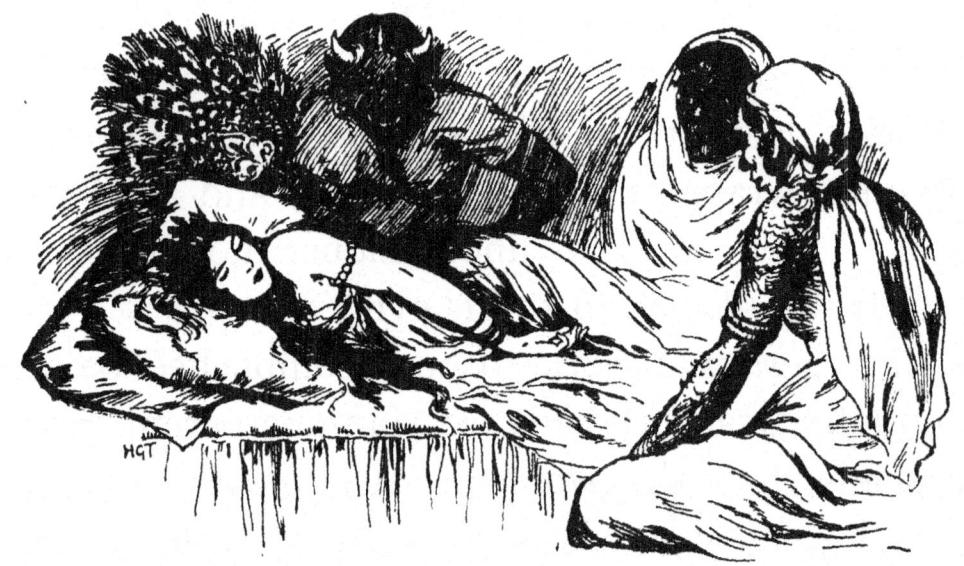

of her gentle sobbing, but he feared to call her name lest he should startle her and thus arouse the suspicion of her guards; so he perched himself by the window and awaited a favourable opportunity of speaking to her.

Dawn was approaching, and as soon as the sun rose there was a noise of trumpets from the palace and soon Ravana came forth in state and proceeded towards the little pavilion.

Sita trembled with terror at the sound of the demon King's footsteps, and she looked vainly around her for a way of escape, but there was none—her demon guards still surrounded her.

" Long have I wooed thee in patience," cried Ravana as he entered the pavilion, " now I ask thee once more. Wilt thou become my bride ? "

" Never," answered Sita firmly. " Leave me in peace, thou evil King."

Ravana pleaded with her for a long while, but his entreaties were of no avail, so he strode out of the pavilion in a furious rage, crying—

" If thou dost continue to reject me, thou shalt surely be put to death."

When Ravana had gone, Sita came to the window, and here, at last, was Hanuman's opportunity.

" Rama," he whispered gently.

Sita gave a violent start, but seeing no one excepting a tiny monkey before her, she thought that she must have dreamed the utterance of that beloved name.

" Rama," whispered Hanuman once more, and he held out a golden ring which Rama had given him, and upon which the name of the Prince was engraven.

At the sight of this token from her husband, Sita nearly swooned with joy and amazement; but Hanuman begged her to control herself, for, should her demon guards notice anything amiss, his plans for her rescue might utterly fail.

So Sita recovered herself with an effort, and her guards, although they observed the little chattering monkey at the window, paid no attention to him, little dreaming that Sita was listening to tidings of most vital importance.

Hanuman promised the captive Princess that he would bring Rama to rescue her without delay, and Sita warned him that an enormous army would be needed to conquer the masses of demons who dwelt in Lanka; then, bidding her not to lose hope, Hanuman departed.

Unfortunately, however, as he was leaving the city he could not restrain his desire to wreak evil upon Ravana, so he resumed his natural size without thinking of the consequences which would follow this rash act, and tearing up huge trees and stones, he hurled them at the walls of Ravana's palace.

Full of wild glee at this work of destruction, Hanuman failed to notice that the demons were rushing to attack him from all directions, and when at last he became conscious of his dangerous position, he seized a marble pillar as a weapon and leaped upon the roof of Ravana's palace.

"Long live Rama!" he cried, dashing his marble club upon the gleaming turrets. "Long live Rama! I am Hanuman, his friend, and I bring ruin upon Ravana and his wicked hosts."

Then Hanuman took a flying leap, trusting that it would land him beyond the reach of his enemies, but, alas! his flight was checked by a swift arrow and he fell to the earth, surrounded by masses of shrieking, revengeful demons.

Hanuman was only slightly wounded, but he was now completely in the power of his enemies. They put him in chains and dragged him before Ravana, who declared that instant death would be too small a punishment for such an insolent intruder.

"Set this spying ape alight," was the King's command, "and let him slowly burn to death."

The demons brought strips of cotton soaked in oil and bound them round Hanuman's tail; then they set fire to these rags and stood by to gloat over the poor ape's torture.

When Hanuman felt his tail alight, he grew desperate, for he realised that owing to his foolish impulse he had now lost all chances of rescuing Sita, and, as the flames mounted higher, he prayed

earnestly to Agui, the God of Fire, imploring him to put out the flames so that Sita might yet be saved.

It seemed, then, as if Agui listened to this petition with favour, for instead of leaping higher now, the flames gradually died away until only the tip of Hanuman's tail remained alight.

As his tortured body grew cooler, Hanuman burst his bonds with a mighty effort, and he leaped away from his astonished enemies, lashing his tail to and fro and setting fire to everything that it happened to touch.

Before the demons had time to realise what Hanuman was doing, their beautiful city burst into flames, and, amidst the general terror and confusion, Hanuman escaped, still dealing destruction wherever he went.

He fled swiftly to the brink of the ocean and extinguished the fire at his tail, then he was about to leap once more over the surging waters when an icy fear gripped his heart. What if Sita were to perish in the burning city !

Without waiting an instant, Hanuman rushed back to the pavilion where, to his infinite relief, Sita still remained ; and after warning her to keep far away from the flames, he returned to the seashore and, with one powerful spring, recrossed the ocean in search of Rama.

PART IV
RAVANA DEFEATED

SWIFT as the wind Hanuman sped back to Kishkinda, and Rama's joy knew no bounds when he heard that Sita was alive and unharmed ; but Hanuman warned him that the rescue of the captive Princess must inevitably be fraught with grave dangers and difficulties, for, unless the fury of the ocean waves were to subside, it would be impossible to land large forces at Lanka.

King Sugriva was quite willing to give Rama a huge army, and the Vanars came forward in millions, rejoicing at the opportunity of attacking their old enemies the demons ; but, when these mighty forces led by Rama, Lakshman and Hanuman had marched to the southern coast, they found that the ocean was still raging furiously, and it seemed to poor Rama as if the rescue of Sita were as far off as ever.

But help was forthcoming to the Vanar armies from an unexpected source—from Lanka itself, strange to relate !

Ever since the flight of Hanuman, the demons had been sorely troubled, for they realised that Lanka, their stronghold, was no longer in-accessible to their enemies, and if *one* Vanar alone could wreak such destruction upon their fair city, they thought, what would happen if an army of these creatures were to land upon the island ?

Ravana felt certain that Rama, aided by Hanuman, would make a desperate effort to rescue Sita now, so the demon King held counsel with his warriors as to the best means of defending the city in case an attack should be made upon it.

Some of the demon chiefs begged Ravana to slay Sita (who was the cause of all the trouble), and then to sally forth with such a mighty army that Rama and his forces must be overthrown ; others urged that the wisest course would be to remain within the city ; but Vibhishan, who was a younger brother of Ravana and who had grown weary of the King's evil ways, implored Ravana to restore Sita to her husband, and thus prevent warfare between demons and Vanars.

However, Ravana was furiously angry at this suggestion, and such a violent quarrel ensued between the two brothers, that Vibhishan, determining to be a party no longer to the infamous schemes of Ravana, took instant flight from Lanka. The demons were able to cross the ocean without any difficulty, so, to the amazement of the Vanars, who were encamped upon the sea-shore, Vibhishan suddenly appeared in their midst and begged to be allowed to join their forces.

" I am weary of Ravana's tyranny and evil-doing," he cried to Rama, " and fain would I help thee to recover thy Sita, for thou hast been cruelly wronged."

At first the Vanars thought that Vibhishan had come to them as a spy, but Rama felt sure that the demon Prince's offer of friendship was sincere, and he asked him how the Vanar armies could reach Lanka, since not one amongst them, excepting Hanuman, was strong enough to leap over the waters.

" A bridge must be built for them," answered Vibhishan. " Let the most powerful apes amongst thy forces cast great rocks and mighty tree-trunks into the ocean, and thou wilt see that in this manner will a causeway be made for thine armies."

Difficult as this advice sounded, it was immediately followed by thousands of great Vanars, who worked unceasingly. They uprooted tree-trunks and tore colossal rocks from the cliffs and mountains, and when these objects were cast into the sea, they began to form a bridge which in five days' time reached as far as the shores of Lanka.

Then, during the night, Rama led the Vanar forces over the causeway, and they landed in safety at Lanka, where they encamped at some distance from the city.

Ravana noted the approach of the enemy from a watch-tower in his palace, and when he beheld the strength of the Vanar forces he was filled with dismay. Hastily rousing his sleeping hosts, he ordered them to make ready for battle without delay, and at daybreak the demon King sallied forth from the city with myriads of fierce warriors.

Now began the most furious fighting that

Vanars and Demons had ever experienced. Rama's forces were armed with great stones and uprooted tree-trunks, which they hurled with all their might against the enemy; but, although countless demons were slain in this manner, it seemed as if their ranks were never thinned. The brave Vanars suffered grievously from the poisoned spears and arrows which the demons wielded, and, at the end of the first day's fighting, Lakshman was wounded nigh unto death. Fortunately good Hanuman was at hand to administer healing herbs to the injured Prince, and Lakshman was soon able to take his place amongst the Vanar chiefs again.

For many days and nights the terrible fighting continued, and first of all it seemed as if Ravana and his hosts would surely triumph, but gradually the tide of fortune began to turn in favour of Rama. One by one, Ravana's most powerful warriors fell before the magic arrows of Rama, until the demon·King resolved, in desperation, to compel Kumbhakarna, his one remaining brother, to enter the fray.

Now Kumbhakarna was the strongest of all the demons, for his stature was that of an enormous giant. Unfortunately he had always been the source of much trouble to Ravana, since, when he moved, his unwieldy limbs were apt to cause much damage in beautiful Lanka, and his appetite was so voracious that it could never be appeased. Therefore Ravana had compelled the poor giant to pass his days in slumber, and only twice a year was he allowed to waken and enjoy a few hours' freedom.

It was not the proper season for Kumbhakarna to be awakened now, but Ravana gave orders that the giant should be roused instantly and informed of the desperate straits at which the demon armies had arrived.

The wakening of Kumbhakarna, however, was a hard task, for though the demons clapped their hands and shouted loudly in the giant's apartment, he did not move, neither did his peaceful snoring cease when brazen trumpets were sounded in his ears. Elephants and camels were then brought into the vast chamber and lashed with sticks until they howled with pain, but still Kumbhakarna slept on, and it was not until the animals were driven over his great body that he stirred and asked in a drowsy tone—

"Why am I wakened before the appointed time?"

The demons hastily explained why they had been bidden to rouse him, whereupon Kumbhakarna growled—

"Ravana hath done ill to anger Rama and these Vanars, nevertheless will I march against them."

So after he had refreshed himself with enormous quantities of meats and wines, Kumbhakarna stumbled out to battle.

The appearance of this huge giant caused quite a panic amongst the Vanars, thousands of whom perished at the hand of this dread demon; but Rama advanced fearlessly with his magic bow which the old sage Agastya had given him, and, to the joy of the Vanars, he sent an arrow right through the heart of Kumbhakarna.

The giant fell to earth, crushing countless demons

beneath his dead body; but now the greatest trial of Rama was to come.

Ravana hastily armed himself with all the deadly weapons at his command and rushed upon the Prince with howls of rage and defiance. Rama managed to withstand the poisoned darts and spears of his enemy, but it seemed, alas! as if his own magic weapons had lost their power, for arrow after arrow he aimed at Ravana, yet still the demon king remained unscathed.

But at last, just as his strength and endurance were beginning to fail him, victory came to Rama.

One arrow, keener than the rest, found its way to the heart of Ravana, who perished instantly amidst the wailing of his hosts.

It seemed now as if the heavens themselves were rejoicing at the death of Ravana, for music sounded in the air, blossoms were showered upon the battlefield by unseen hands, and, in the ears of weary Rama, sweet voices breathed the words—

" Champion of Gods and mortals, thou hast done well ! "

With the death of their King, the hostility of the demons vanished, and, laying down their arms, they surrendered to the conquering Vanars.

14

Rama immediately proclaimed Vibhishan as ruler of Lanka, then the eager Prince hastened in search of his wife.

Sita was alone in her pavilion, for her terrified guardians had fled from her long since. When she heard the sound of footsteps, she looked up in fear lest Ravana had come to molest her; but catching sight of Rama, she rushed forward and fell into his arms amidst tears of joy.

At first Rama and Sita could hardly believe that their cruel separation was at an end, but the happy thought soon occurred to the Prince that his beloved wife was restored to him at the very moment when his sentence of banishment from Ayodhya had expired.

When good Hanuman heard this, he insisted upon hastening to Ayodhya, so that he might inform Prince Bharat that Rama and Sita were about to return to the city, and Vibhishan, who had quickly established order amongst the routed demons, brought forth a wonderful chariot which he placed at the disposal of the joyful Prince and Princess.

Then Rama and Sita stepped into the flower-covered car drawn by swans, and took leave of Vibhishan, who remained at Lanka and governed his dominion so wisely and benevolently that,

CATCHING SIGHT OF RAMA SHE RUSHED FORWARD
From "The Adventures of Rama and Sita"

henceforth, the demons ceased to trouble the peace of Gods and mortals.

The swans flew through the air with the flower chariot, and after a joyous and speedy journey, Rama and Sita arrived at Ayodhya, to find the inhabitants of the city frantic with delight at their return.

Prince Bharat was delighted to give the reins of government into the hands of his brother, and, amidst splendid preparations, the coronation of Rama and Sita took place at last. There was no jealous soul to mar the ceremony this time, for Manthara was dead, and Queen Kaikeyi, who had long since repented of her evil deeds, besought the forgiveness of Rama, which was readily granted to her.

Lakshman was greatly honoured for his faithfulness to Rama, and good Hanuman returned to Kishkinda, laden with costly gifts for himself and his king, Sugriva ; but what the noble ape valued far more than gold and jewels, was the thought of the love and gratitude which Rama and Sita had vowed ever to bear him.

Thus ended the wanderings of Rama and Sita, for their reign, which lasted many years, was filled with peace and happiness. Through their good example, there was joy and prosperity in the land

of Kosala, since each man loved his neigh-
bour as himself.   Not only was there contentment
amongst mortals, however, but the Gods themselves rejoiced that sorrow and sin had vanished
from the land with the death of dread Ravana.

THE CURSE OF KALI

NALA, the King of Nishadha, was well beloved by his subjects. He was young and handsome, a wise and just ruler ; he was skilled in all the arts and sciences and there was none throughout India to match him as a charioteer. In fact, he had only one fault—a love of gambling, which cost him dearly, as you will hear later on.

Now, in the neighbouring country of Vidarbha, the king's daughter, Damayanti, was reputed to be the most beautiful maiden in the world. She had countless suitors but whenever her father urged her to accept one of them, she would reply firmly : " Dear father, I will only wed the man I love, and as yet I have never seen him."

After a while the King of Vidarbha lost patience and announced that he was going to arrange a Swayamvara for his daughter. Damayanti sorrowed at this, for a Swayamvara was a festival at which suitors presented themselves and where one of them must be chosen as a bridegroom. No maiden was allowed to remain unwed after a Swayamvara had been held in her honour, so

213

poor Damayanti wept in secret at the prospect of being an unwilling bride.

Nala was invited to attend the Swayamvara, and he longed yet feared to present himself before the princess. He had fallen in love with the mere description of her, but he was modest, in spite of all his advantages, and thought he had little chance of success amongst so many suitors.

Shortly before the festival he was strolling by the river when a swan came sailing along. Nala thought how fine such a bird would look upon the lotus-lake in his garden, so he seized the swan by its slender throat and held it fast.

" Let me go, Nala," cried the bird piteously.

" Have no fear," answered the king. " I will not harm you. You shall dwell upon my lotus-lake and have all you desire."

" There is only one thing I desire," the swan said, " and that is my freedom. Give it to me, O king ! and you shall have your heart's desire."

" Go free, then," cried Nala, loosening his hold upon the swan's throat. " Would that I could have my heart's desire so easily ! "

" It shall be granted you," said the grateful bird. " Listen, Nala ! You long to win the heart of the Princess Damayanti. Well, I will fly to Vidarbha, seek the princess and sing your praises in her delicate ear until she must love the very thought of you."

"Away with you then, bird!" cried Nala joyously.

The swan spread his wings and flew without resting until he reached the kingdom of Vidarbha. He found the princess alone in her garden. She had dismissed her attendants, for she wanted to think about her future in solitude. Her lustrous eyes were heavy with weeping and her cheeks were pale, but her beauty was still dazzling to behold. The swan alighted at her feet and sang to her of Nala, of his virtues, his handsome appearance, of his great love for her, and Damayanti listened with her pale cheeks glowing like a rose and her heart beating fast.

"O swan!" she said shyly, "return to this incomparable king and tell him that if he loves me truly I will choose none other at my Swayamvara."

Now, instead of dreading the festival, Damayanti looked forward to it eagerly, for she longed for the sight of Nala. When the great day came, dressed in rich apparel and hung with pearls and shining gems, she sat upon her throne holding a garland of flowers. Powerful kings and princes passed before her, but she kept her head averted until the coming of Nala; then, rising to her feet, she flung her garland around his shoulders. Cries of joy, mingled with murmurs of grief from the rejected suitors, echoed in the vast hall, and Nala was thus proclaimed the favoured bridegroom.

The King of Vidarbha was delighted at his daughter's choice of a husband, and the wedding ceremony took place immediately, after which Nala and his bride set out for the kingdom of Nishadha.

Scarcely had they left the palace when a belated suitor appeared, one called Kali, who was really an evil spirit in the guise of a prince. When he learned that Nala had carried off the prize, Kali's rage knew no bounds, and he laid a solemn curse upon Nala to the effect that when he should next play at dice dire evil should befall him.

Nala knew nothing of this curse, but for a long time after his marriage he forbore to gamble. He was far too happy with Damayanti and the two lovely children who were born to them to think about dice. However, the day came when his younger brother Pushkara challenged him to a game, and as Nala thought it would be discourteous to refuse, he sat down to the table.

Now the curse of Kali began to take effect. All that day Nala lost at every throw; so, thinking his luck must surely change, he insisted upon continuing the game on the morrow. Day after day the gamblers went on playing, in spite of Damayanti's appeal that they should desist, and Nala lost gold and treasure to his brother without winning a single throw himself. At last Damayanti grew fearful for the future of her children, so in charge of a faithful servant she sent them to her father's kingdom.

Still the gambling continued, until Nala had staked and lost his kingdom and rose from the table a ruined man.

Then Pushkara, who had long been jealous of Nala, said spitefully : " You have yet one more thing to stake, brother. Let us play for Damayanti herself."

Nala looked at him in silent scorn, then divesting himself of his crown and all his jewels he walked out of the palace. Before he had gone very far he was joined by Damayanti, who had put on a simple robe without any adornment.

" Dear husband," she cried, " surely you are not leaving me ? Let us both return to my father's kingdom, where our children await us."

But Nala, maddened by his misfortunes and the thought of his unworthiness, replied : " How can I, who came to your father's palace as a powerful king, return there as a beggar ? Go to your father alone, Damayanti, and leave me to my shame."

But Damayanti followed him in spite of his protests, and they wandered into a deep, dark wood on the outskirts of the city. Night fell, and still they walked dejectedly, until Damayanti sank down for very weariness and slept.

Then Nala, crazed by misfortune, said to himself: "If I abandon Damayanti, surely she will return to her father's kingdom, which is a better fate than remaining a beggarly outcast with me."

So, although his heart was well-nigh broken at leaving her, Nala slipped away, and when Damayanti awoke at dawn, she found herself alone in the forest. Thinking he must be within earshot, she cried Nala's name again and again ; then she ran hither and thither but could find no traces of him anywhere. At length the truth dawned upon her. Nala had left her to return to her own people by herself.

The unhappy queen, scarcely knowing what she was doing, wandered deeper and deeper into the forest. Fearsome wild beasts were prowling in all directions, but none came near to harm her. She kept herself alive with wild berries for food, and after many days she came to an open space where a party of merchants were encamped with caravans and horses.

They cried out in surprise at the sight of a beautiful, dishevelled woman, and Damayanti besought them to tell her if they had seen Nala on their travels. The merchants had no good tidings for her, but they happened to be on their way to the kingdom of Vidarbha, so Damayanti, in despair, joined them, and was carried back to her father's palace.

Enraged against Nala, but full of love and pity for their daughter, her parents received Damayanti tenderly and led her to her children, who were playing in happy ignorance of what had befallen. Damayanti rejoiced at the sight of them, but they could not console her for the loss of Nala. She implored her father to send messengers in search of him, so, in order to pacify her, the King of Vidarbha instructed his servants to visit all the neighbouring kingdoms and to cry upon the name of Nala wherever they went.

In the meantime what had happened to the wretched Nala? After he had deserted Damayanti he wandered about aimlessly until he reached the kingdom of Ayodhya, many, many leagues distant from Vidarbha. Passing through a little wood he heard a cry for help and found a snake imprisoned in the trunk of a tree. Now, this snake was really a king of serpents who had incurred the spite of wicked Kali. For that reason he was in a very sorry plight, and he called upon Nala to rescue him. Nala set him free and the snake king thanked him for his great service and asked him how he could serve him.

" Alas ! how can you help such a ruined man ? " cried Nala bitterly, and he told the snake king the story of his misfortunes.

" All this evil must be the work of Kali," said the snake king. " He has cursed you, doubtless, but he shall be outwitted, never fear, if you follow my counsel."

He then told Nala that he must offer his services as chief charioteer to the King of Ayodhya, and after a time all would be well with him ; but he must have patience. To Nala's astonishment the snake king struck him upon the hand with his poison fang, and then bade him look at himself in a streamlet near by.

Nala looked at his reflection in the water and gave a cry of dismay, for he was transformed to a misshapen, ugly individual.

" That is so that none shall recognise you yet," said the snake king, " but here is a magic vest. When the time comes that you wish to reveal yourself, slip on the vest and you will resume your own shape. Follow my instructions faithfully and you shall reign once more over your own people."

Nala thanked the snake king and went on his way with the magic vest in his pocket. He presented himself before the King of Ayodhya, and calling himself Vahuka, asked whether his majesty was in need of a charioteer. The king told him to show what he could do with horses, and was so impressed by the so-called Vahuka's wonderful driving that he engaged him immediately as his chief charioteer.

In spite of Vahuka's unprepossessing appearance the king grew attached to him and learned many things from him concerning the management of horses. In return, being skilled in games, he imparted secret knowledge to Nala as regards the game of dice. One day, when Nala was driving the king along the high road, messengers came by calling upon the name of Nala and relating how his wife Damayanti besought him to return to her.

The king bade his charioteer pull up the horses, and he asked questions of the messengers and then told them that, so far as he knew, there was no one called Nala in his kingdom.

But the messengers had observed the skill of the king's charioteer and how his eyes had filled with tears at the mention of Damayanti's name. So they hastened back to Vidarbha and sought the presence of the sorrowful queen.

" O lady ! " they cried, " we have seen no one like Nala on our travels, but in the kingdom of Ayodhya there is a crooked, hideous charioteer whose skill with horses equals that of your husband. Moreover, he wept at the sound of your name. Yet he cannot possibly be Nala, who was the straightest and handsomest of men, whereas this charioteer is hunchbacked and has a most ill-favoured countenance."

Damayanti pondered over these tidings. Was it possible that Nala could have altered in such an extraordinary manner ? Perchance privation and suffering might have changed him thus. In her heart she felt that this charioteer must be her husband, but how was she to discover the truth ? She besought her father then to invite the King of Ayodhya to visit him and to bring his most skilled charioteer so that he might compare his prowess with that of the champion driver of Vidarbha.

The King of Ayodhya accepted the invitation and bade Nala drive him to Vidarbha. Nala, longing yet dreading to visit the home of his wife, accomplished the journey with incredible swiftness.

When the chariot drew up before the palace Damayanti was waiting with her father to greet the royal visitor. She looked at the charioteer and her heart sank. No, this ugly creature was not Nala, and yet no one else could have driven so quickly. She spoke gentle words to the charioteer and asked him if he had seen her husband, perchance. Nala longed to reveal himself, but the sense of shame still kept him silent. Then Damayanti sent for her children, and in front of the charioteer spoke of their fatherless state and wept. Now, Nala could control himself no longer. He donned his magic suit and, resuming his own form immediately, he knelt at the feet of Damayanti and implored her forgiveness. He told her how his misfortunes had been effected by the curse of Kali, and Damayanti embraced him and wept again, but this time for very joy.

When tidings of this reunion were spread through the kingdom there was much rejoicing at the return of Nala. The King of Vidarbha begged him to remain there with his wife and children but Nala answered : " I will return to Nishadha, and maybe I shall win back my kingdom, for surely the curse has been lifted from me."

So Nala set out for Nishadha, and on his arrival he came before Pushkara and challenged him to a game of dice, the stake this time to be the life of either of them.

Pushkara consented to play, for he thought Nala would surely lose the throw. Breathlessly the brothers threw, and Pushkara lost.

Then Nala said: "O Pushkara! I will not exact the penalty of your life, but give me back my kingdom and all my possessions and you shall go free wherever you will."

So once more Nala reigned over the people of Nishadha, and lived happily with his beloved wife and children.

But never, never again could he be induced to gamble with the dice, and no more was he troubled by the ill-will of the wicked Kali.

THE HARE IN THE MOON

WHEN, on a clear night, English children look up at the bright moon, they think they can see marked on it, the figure of a man with a bundle of faggots in his hand, and by his side a dog. But to the eyes of Indian children the dog seems more like a hare, and if they ask how the mark came there, this is the story their mothers tell them.

Thousands of years ago, when animals could talk, and the moon's face was as clear as a sheet of paper, there lived in a certain wood, four wise creatures—a hare, a jackal, an otter, and a monkey.

They were great friends, and, after the labours of the day were over, they would meet together to give and take good advice. The hare was the noblest and wisest of the four, and he was never tired of telling the others tales of virtue, and recommending them to observe all the laws which were obeyed by good men and women.

One evening, after examining the moon's face very carefully, he said to his friends—

" To-morrow good men will observe a fast, for

I perceive it will be the middle day of the month. They will eat no food until sunset, and during the day they will not deny alms to any beggar or priest who asks them. Let us vow to each other to do the same, thus elevating ourselves towards the dignity of human beings." The others agreed, and then separated to their own dwelling-places for the night.

Next day the otter rose early and thought to himself: " If I keep this vow, how very hungry I shall be by the evening ! I had better have a good meal ready for myself ; " and he set out towards the river. Now it happened that a fisherman had caught seven large red fishes a few hours before ; had strung them together with twine, and buried them in the sand ; then he had rowed higher up the stream in search of more, meaning to come back later on to fetch his hidden haul.

This fish the otter soon smelt out. " Ha ! ha ! " he thought, " a supper all ready prepared for me ! But, since it is a holy day, I will not really steal it ; " and he called out—not very loudly—" Does any one claim this fish ? " Of course there was no answer, so in high glee he carried it back to his home and, setting it aside ready for the evening, he lay down to sleep away the hours of fast, secure from the possibility of being asked alms by any beggar or priest.

Much the same thoughts passed through the minds of the jackal and monkey, when they awoke that morning and remembered their vows. The jackal, after searching for an hour or so, found a cooked lizard and a bowl of milk-curd in a peasant's hut ; and the monkey, without searching at all, climbed a tree and picked a bunch of

HGT

mangoes. Well pleased at the idea of their evening feast, each retired with his food to his lair, and, like the otter, lay down to sleep, secure from interruption.

The hare woke up with the sun, and, shaking his long ears, came out from his burrow and sniffed the dewy grass. " I need not grudge my day's fast," he said aloud, " since, when evening comes,

I can eat my fill of this delicious herbage which grows here so plentifully. But, alas! if any beggar or priest comes across me and demands alms, what can I give? I cannot offer him grass, and I have no possessions. I must offer myself. I have heard that men regard the flesh of hare as very good to eat;" and, with a contented mind, he scampered off in search of adventure.

Now the God Sakka was sitting in a cloud upon the top of a mountain not far away, and he heard the little creature's resolve. " I will test him," said he. " Surely no hare can be so noble and unselfish as all this!" So, when evening approached, he descended from the cloud, and, assuming the form of an old priest, he sat down by the side of the hare's burrow, and, on the animal's approach, addressed him: " Good evening, little creature. Can you direct me where to find food, for I have fasted all day and am now so hungry that I cannot pray."

The hare, remembering his vow, answered: " Good evening, sir priest. Is it true that men eat and relish the flesh of my race?"

" Quite true," said the seeming priest.

" Then, as I have no other food to offer you, and can direct you to none, take and relish me."

" But I may not slay any animal with my hands because it is a holy day, and I am a holy man."

" Then collect faggots and set them alight. I will leap into the flames myself, and when I am roasted you can eat me."

Sakka marvelled as he heard this, but still not wholly convinced, he caused a fire of coals to spring magically out of the earth, whereupon the hare, without hesitation, jumped into the middle of the flames.

" What has happened, good priest ?" he called out in a few moments. "The fire roars round me, but not a hair of my coat is singed; even my whiskers cannot feel the slightest heat."

As he spoke the fire died down, and he found himself crouching not upon ashes or smouldering cinders, but upon the cool sweet grass, while, instead of the old priest, there stood beside him the form of a radiant God, who spoke in bell-like tones—

" I am the God Sakka, little hare, and having heard your vow, I wished to test its sincerity. Such unselfishness as yours is worth an immortal reward.   See ! you shall have it."

Sakka then stretched out his hand towards the mountain, and drew from it some of the juice which ran in its veins. This he threw upwards towards the moon, which had just risen, and instantly the outline of the hare was painted upon her silver surface.

" For ever and ever, little hare," continued the God, " shall you look down from heaven upon the world, to remind men of the old truth, ' Give to others, and the Gods will give to you.' "

The hare looked up and pricked his ears towards his new looking-glass ; but when he turned to thank Sakka, nobody was there. The God had gone back to his cloud. So he set contentedly to work upon his supper, and presently went down to his burrow and slept, full of grass and gladness.

THE BOY WHO COULD SEE FOOTSTEPS

ABOUT twenty miles away from the city of Benares, there once dwelt, in a dark but spacious cave, by the side of the road, a creature called a Yakka. She had the face of a horse and the body of a woman; she was strong and fierce as a tigress; and she lived upon the flesh of any men or beasts whom she could entrap.

One day the Yakka caught a Brahman who was travelling alone towards Benares, and carried him with incredible swiftness into her cavern. When she saw that he was young and handsome she asked him whether, if she spared his life, he would marry her; and he, thinking that of two evils this would be the less, agreed to become her

231

husband. Afterwards the Yakka grew more and more humane and gentle, gave up eating like a cannibal, and tried in all sorts of ways to refine her habits and mind. However, she always feared that the Brahman would run away from her if he could, so she used to roll a huge stone in front of the entrance to the cave, before she went out to forage for food, and in this way the poor priest was kept penned like a slave in his prison. The Yakka was happy enough, and spent her days lying in wait for passing caravans from which she would, either by stealth or threats, obtain wine, spices and fruits, and upon these she and her husband lived. At length a little son was born to them, who speedily grew into a stalwart and clever lad, in spite of his being always cooped up in the dark, cold cave. The Yakka became devoted to him, and doubled her attentions to make his father comfortable and happy. But the poor Brahman pined for freedom, and would no doubt soon have died of melancholy had he not been helped by his little son, who one day said to him—

" Father, why is my mother's face so different from ours ? "

" Because she is an Ogress, Son, and we are men."

" Then why do we live with her in this dark
hovel, instead of among our fellows ? "

" Because of the great stone which the Yakka
rolls in front of the cave's entrance ; it is too heavy
for me to remove, else I had long since fled from
this prison."

The Boy no sooner heard this, than he sprang
up, and setting his shoulder to the stone, easily
rolled it aside. As quickly as might be, he then
seized his father by the hand, and they ran until
the Brahman, unused to the light and air, became
half blind and dizzy with his unaccustomed
exertion ; and even the Boy was breathless. But,
alas ! before they had recovered sufficiently to go
on again, they heard the thud of the Ogress's feet
in pursuit, and she soon came up to them.

" Oh, thankless husband, and more thankless
child ! " she cried. " Why do you flee away ?
What did you lack in my cavern that the heart of
man could desire ? Did you not lie upon beds of
leaf and moss ? Did you not drink wine and eat
dates ? "

" Mother," answered the Boy, " we lacked air
and light, and these are more necessary to men
even than wine and dates."

" Come back with me, and you shall have both,"
she said. So perforce they returned, and she broke

the great stone into splinters, and allowed them to wander into the woods and up and down the road ; but whenever they got more than a mile away from the cavern they would always hear her great feet thudding after them.

One day the Boy found out that his Mother's power extended only as far as the river one way, two leagues distant, and as far as the mountains the other way, three leagues distant. So when she was fast asleep, on a dark night, he and his father crept out of the cave, and fled for dear life towards the river. They had just managed to reach the bank when the noise of pursuit became audible ; but the Boy did not pause—he hoisted his father on his back, and waded up to his waist in the stream. Then, safe beyond the Ogress's power, turned his head.

" Come back ! come back ! " she wailed.

" Never," replied the Boy. " We are men, and it is right that we should dwell with our own kind."

The Yakka knelt upon the river bank, and wept tears into the running water ; but as she saw she could not recover the truants, who had by now made their way to the other bank, she at length ceased her complaints, and because she loved her child greatly, she told him he should take from

HE DEMANDED AN AUDIENCE OF THE GRAND VIZIER
From "The Boy who could see Footsteps"

her a talisman that should prove of much value to him in the world of men.

" Take this stone," she said, throwing it across to him, " and hang it about your neck. By its power you will be able to perceive footsteps even twelve years after they have been made upon the ground by the feet of men."

The Boy caught the stone, and, carefully fastening it round his neck, thanked her ; then, waving adieus, he and his father proceeded on their way towards Benares. As soon as he arrived in the city, he went straight to the King's palace, and demanded an audience of the Grand Vizier, whom he informed that he had the power of seeing footsteps.

" Should any robber tamper with the King's treasury, I can trace the thief and find the jewels," he announced. " Will your honour inquire of your royal master, whether he will take me into service ? "

The King was overjoyed to do so, for he was extremely rich and miserly, and lived in daily and nightly fear of being robbed.

" How much does the lad expect us to pay him ? " he inquired.

" A thousand rupees daily, sire," answered the Vizier ; at which the King at first demurred, but, the Boy standing out for that sum, he at length agreed to it.

Some months passed, and, as the fame of the Boy's reputed gift had travelled through all Benares, no attempts were made to rob the treasury.

At length the King called the Vizier to him and said—

" How are we to know that this Boy is not an impostor ? Here do we pay him a thousand rupees daily, and in return, for all I can see, he does nothing but sit upon a rug near the marble

fountain, with his old father, playing at chess and drinking scented water. Methinks I am being cheated by the lad. Let us therefore rob the treasury ourselves, and test this power he boasts of."

The Vizier consented, and the next night the two thieves broke into the vaults where the treasure was concealed, took many jewels and much money, which they placed in sacks ; and with the booty walked three times round the palace, traversed the gardens, climbed over the wall by means of a ladder, and finally reaching a tank in the midst of a meadow dropped the sacks into it, and returned by the same route to the palace.

Next day the King raised a terrible outcry. Some of the most precious of the crown jewels had been stolen ! The thief must be found ! Where was the Boy who could see Footsteps ?

" Here I am, sire," said he, hastening to the audience chamber, as soon as wind of the burglary reached him. " Let me at once trace the thief." And he proceeded, starting from the vaults, to walk three times round the palace, to traverse the gardens, to climb over the wall at a certain spot, by means of a ladder, and finally reaching a tank in the midst of a meadow, he ordered a diver to descend into the water, and bring up whatever he should find at the bottom.

" I have seen the footsteps of two men all the way," he said, " and they are men of distinction," for he knew very well by the shape of the steps—which corresponded exactly with those the King and Vizier were now making—who the thieves were.

But he loyally kept silence, for how dismayed the courtiers would be to find that the thieves were no other than the King and his own Grand Vizier!

For some moments there was deep silence as they all stood breathlessly around gazing down into the tank.

The courtiers clapped, huzzaed, and waved their caps as the diver brought up, one by one, the bags full of treasure ; but the King, who had secretly been disappointed to see how well the boy was earning his salary, now whispered to the Vizier : " This is all very well ; he has recovered the lost property, but who can tell whether he is able to trace the thieves ?   I will test him further ; " and, turning to the lad, he said aloud—

" Now find me these thieves."

" Nay, sire, that is of no consequence now that the jewels are recovered," answered the Boy. He did not wish to expose the King's trickery before his subjects, rightly feeling that they could no longer respect a sovereign who played the thief himself, and acted a part so full of lies.

But the King insisted. " I shall not be willing to pay you so big a salary if you cannot find the thieves, for, by my sword and turban, my heart longs to punish the rascals."

" Beware, O King, of your words," cried the Boy, still anxious to protect his sovereign. " If he upon whom the people depend, fail them, lie to them, play the thief to them, what shall the people do ? "

The King laughed ; and was so foolish that he did not see how clearly he was being warned.

" The people should punish such an one," was all he said.

" Shall I name the thieves, then ? " asked the Boy for the last time.

" Yes, or else I cut your thousand rupees daily down to a hundred."

" Yourself and your Vizier, O King ! You are the thieves ! "

And when the courtiers and people learned that their ruler had stooped to all this trickery, acting the part of knave and fool in company with his chief statesman, in order, if he might, to reduce a salary he could well afford to pay, they decided that he was not worthy to hold a position of trust over them ; so they dethroned and exiled him, and gave the crown to the Boy who could see Footsteps.

THE KING'S COLUMN

THERE was once a King living in Benares, who was ambitious to build himself a palace more remarkable than any other in India. He could not make it richer, taller, stronger or more beautiful without immense expense and trouble ; so he decided to create its novelty by supporting the entire structure upon one column only—though whether it was to be shaped like a dove-cot or not, I cannot possibly tell you.

He called his Vizier to him and said, " Send men to my forests far and near, and bid them hew down and bring to the city without delay the most stalwart tree they can find."

The Vizier at once despatched thirty foresters, who soon returned, saying that though there were many trees equally strong and gigantic in the King's woods, they could never carry or drag them over so much difficult country as lay between the forests and the city.

When the King heard this, he summoned the foresters. " By means of horses, one of these trees must be brought," he said to them.

" It is not possible, O most mighty sire," they answered. " No horses could move such a tree an inch."

" By means of oxen, then," he said.

" It is less possible, O most illustrious ruler ; the oxen could not force their way through such miles of close wood."

" By means of elephants, then."

" It is less and less possible, O most enlightened and revered lord ; for the ground is so marshy that the elephants would sink to the knees in it."

" Very well," said the King angrily. " You must find me a tree just as big, in one of my own parks, and bring it hither within seven days."

The foresters departed, and went directly to a splendid sal-tree which grew not far from the palace, and was worshipped by the people of many villages round about, because within it dwelt a God, and it was he who gave to the tree its unusual strength, size, and beauty.

So when the foresters had decided, with much reluctance, that the King's column must be made from this lordly sal-tree and from no other, they came with garlands, lamps and music to sacrifice to the God inside, and to warn him that he must leave his abode, for within seven days it would be cut to the ground.

They lit their lamps and placed them in a circle round the tree ; they hung their garlands upon the branches, and tied nosegays among the leaves ; then some of them, joining hands, danced, others made music upon lutes and zitherns, and yet others sang—

> " With cruel axe and saw we come
>   To hew this trunk, thy age-long home ;
>   Us, who dance about the tree-God,
>   Punish not, benignant tree-God,
>   At our King's commandment we
>   Bid thee listen, fear, and flee."

The tree-God heard, and understood well enough what was about to happen. He remained quiet as a resting breeze for a few moments, and then all his leaves began to whisper and his topmost branches bowed ; so the foresters went away satisfied that he had answered their song. Now this was what the leaves were whispering to each other—

" Sh—sh—should this King's decision hold, not only shall we perish, we and our spirit—for the sal-God cannot exist anywhere else—but our fall will crush all the little sal-trees that have sprung up and thrive under our protection. For ourselves we care not, but for the children's sake we wish the King had not wished what he did wish

—sh—sh—sh." And so the whispering died away.

The sal-God within the tree thought, "This must not be allowed. I must visit the King and persuade him."

That night, while the King was asleep, a glorious shining figure appeared to him in his dreams, and spoke in a voice that was like a rustle—

"I am the God of the sal-tree, O King. Thy foresters this day have told me of thy purpose to fell me. I have come to beg thee to reverse thy decree."

"Nay, I cannot," answered the King. "Yours is the only tree in all my parks strong enough to support by itself a palace, and therefore I must have it."

"Consider, O King! For sixty thousand years have I been worshipped by the people of many villages, and never has aught but benefit gone out from me to them. The birds nest in me; I send a vast and most lovely shade upon the grass beneath me; against my trunk do men rest and creatures rub themselves, glad of the coolness. The earth blesses me."

"True, all true enough, good sal-God, but for all this I cannot spare you. My will is unshaken."

"I AM THE GOD OF THE SAL-TREE, O KING. THY FORESTERS
HAVE TOLD ME OF THY PURPOSE TO FELL ME"

245

Then the tree-God sank his head **upon his** breast and sorrowfully spoke.

"Then, mighty King, grant me one last request. Let me be felled in three parts: first my head, with its crown of waving greenery; next my middle, with its hundred strong arms and hands; last my base, which bears the heaviest and knottiest of my limbs upon it."

"This is a strange request," said the King.

"Never before did I hear of one who desired

three times to suffer the death stroke. Why not endure the anguish but once, and have it over? Give your reason."

"It is thus, then. Round about me have grown up my family. Dozens of young sal-trees have sprung from me, and thrived in my generous shadow. Should you fell me with one mighty stroke, my weight would certainly crush all my children to death ; but if I three times suffer the stroke, and fall in three pieces, some of the little ones may escape. Is my prayer granted ? "

" Indeed it is," said the King, whereupon the tree-God faded into nothingness.

The next morning the King, calling his Vizier and his foresters to him, told them that his mind had changed, and that the column for the new palace should be built of stone, not wood, " For," said he, " within the sal-tree dwells a spirit nobler than my own ; " and he told them of his vision, and they all marvelled.

FROM
" SAKUNTALA,
OR THE
RING
OF
REMEMBRANCE "

248

CPSIA information can be obtained
at www.ICGtesting.com
Printed in the USA
BVOW04*1420020118
504220BV00008B/31/P